D0204914

CAESAR
DE BELLO GALLICO I

CAESAR

DE BELLO GALLICO I

Edited with Introduction,
Notes and Vocabulary by

Colin Ewan

Bristol Classical Press

This impression 2003
This edition published in 1993 by
Bristol Classical Press
an imprint of
Gerald Duckworth & Co. Ltd.
90-93 Cowcross Street, London EC1M 6BF
Tel: 020 7490 7300
Fax: 020 7490 0080
inquiries@duckworth-publishers.co.uk
www.ducknet.co.uk

First published in 1957 by G. Bell & Sons Ltd
© 1957 by Bell & Hyman Ltd

A catalogue record for this book is available
from the British Library

ISBN 0 86292 177 5

Printed and bound in Great Britain by
Biddles Ltd, *www.biddles.co.uk*

PREFACE

THIS edition of the first book of Caesar's *Gallic War* has been prepared on the same lines as other editions of Caesar in the Alpha Classics. In the Introduction and Index of Names, sufficient 'background' information is given to enable students to understand something of the Roman world of Caesar's time, of the general history of the period as it affected Rome, and of Gaul itself and the Romans' interest in Gaul. The maps are drawn to illustrate this background, and to make the text clear. The Notes aim chiefly at explaining the narrative, and at elucidating the more difficult passages, noteworthy points of syntax being so far as possible related to first principles. Many authorities have been consulted on many points, but particularly Rice Holmes, *Caesar's Conquest of Gaul*; Jullian, *Histoire de la Gaule*; Grose-Hodge, *Roman Panorama*; Adcock, *Caesar as Man of Letters*; Brogan, *Roman Gaul* and the *Cambridge Ancient History*—and to all these grateful acknowledgment is made. Thanks are also due to the Oxford University Press for permission to use the text of Du Pontet in the *Oxford Classical Texts*. In eight places, this text has been altered (mostly by the omission of a doubtful word or words) to remove unnecessary difficulties, these alterations being mentioned in footnotes.

C. E.

September, 1956

CONTENTS

LIST OF ILLUSTRATIONS

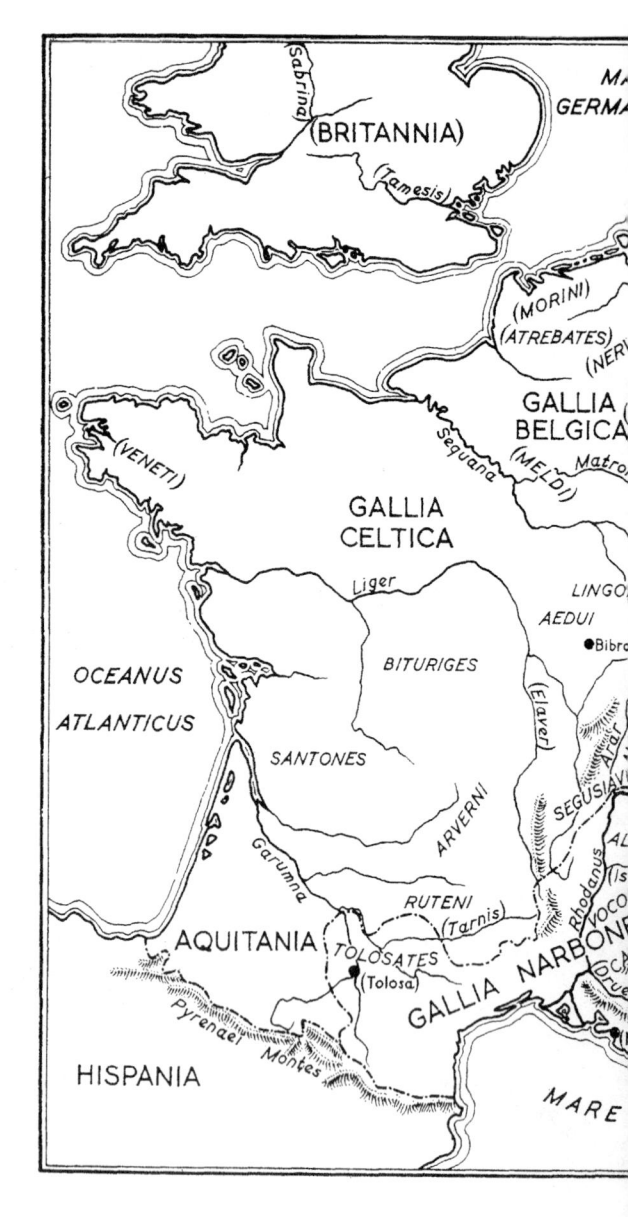

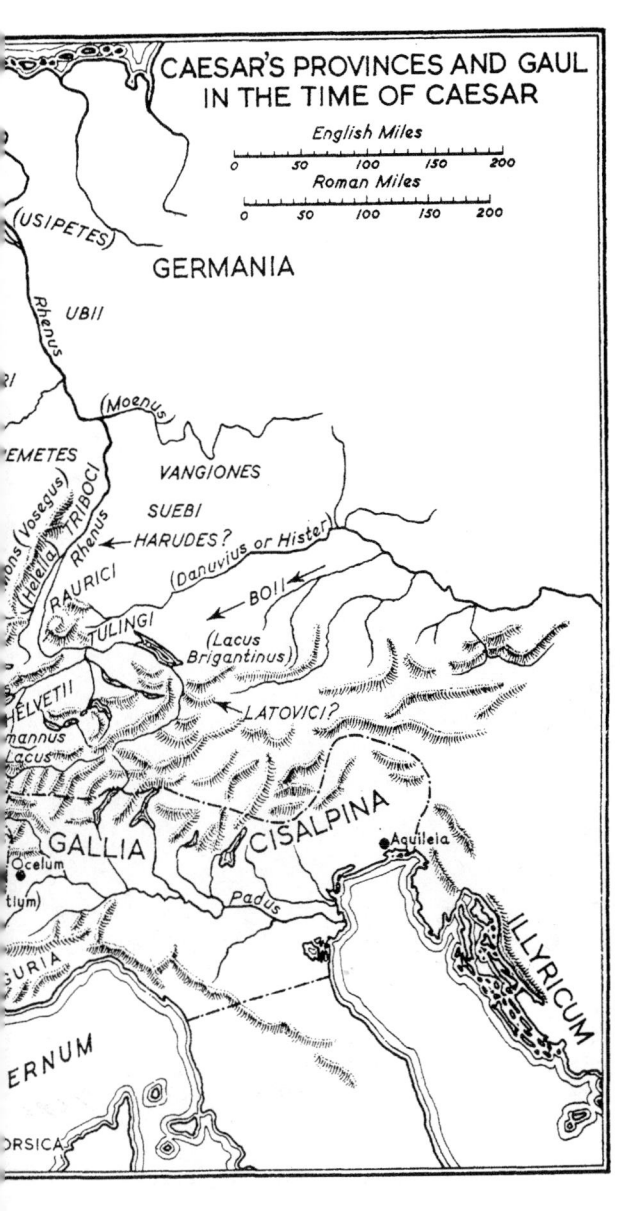

CAESAR'S PROVINCES AND GAUL
IN THE TIME OF CAESAR

English Miles
0   50   100   150   200

Roman Miles
0   50   100   150   200

(USIPETES)

GERMANIA

Rhenus

UBII

RI

(Moenus)

EMETES

VANGIONES

SUEBI

ons (Vosegus)
HARUDES?

Rhenus

TRIBOCI

(Helela)

(Danuvius or Hister)

RAURICI

BOII

TULINGI

(Lacus
Brigantinus)

HELVETII

LATOVICI?

mannus
Lacus

CISALPINA

GALLIA

Aquileia

Ocelum

Padus

tium)

ILLYRICUM

URIA

ERNUM

ORSICA

INTRODUCTION

I. Caesar's Governorship in Gaul, and his Commentaries on the Gallic War

Caesar was consul in 59 B.C. During this year, a tribune, P. Vatinius, passed a law which made Caesar governor, as proconsul, of Cisalpine Gaul (Gaul-south-of-the-Alps—roughly, Lombardy) and Illyricum, for five years, till the end of 54 B.C. Before he took up this command, he was given also Transalpine Gaul. The tenure of his command was later extended to 49 B.C. By 51 B.C., he had completely subdued Gaul, after seven years of constant fighting. In that year, he published the seven books of his Commentaries, which tell the story down to the end, in 52 B.C., of the revolt led by the great Arvernian, Vercingetorix; the last stages of his Gallic command were related in the eighth book, written after his death by his friend Aulus Hirtius.

The first book tells of the two campaigns he fought during the summer and early autumn of the first year of his command. In these campaigns, he repelled and broke two dangerous invasions from the East: the first, of the Helvetii, a Celtic people from Switzerland; the second, of a mixed host of German tribes, led by Ariovistus.

II. Rome and her Empire

In 59 B.C., Rome governed virtually the whole of Southern Europe, from Spain to the Black Sea. She ruled the islands of the Mediterranean, with important footholds on the North African coastland. This vast expansion had come as the result of more than two centuries of constant wars, in which she had overcome every opponent. In many cases these wars, and the conquests that followed them, were forced on her. The Empire was still growing, though again and again those who governed her were reluctant to accept fresh increases.

The truth is that, at this time, the Roman system of government was out of date. It was still fitted to a pattern established when Rome was a small city-state. The chief officials were elected at Rome, each year, by voters amongst whom the influence of the city-dwellers was supreme. The chief deliberative body, the Senate, was like a Roman city-council, as it had been for centuries, and was recruited from those elected to the high offices of state. Provincial governors were those who had held office at Rome, and they often regarded their governorship as a means to grow rich. In spite of these handicaps, such was the Roman genius for organisation, such was the quality of her leaders, and such her superiority over all competitors, that the Empire continued to exist, and continued to grow.

Side by side with this condition of external affairs, there were vast difficulties within Italy and in Rome herself. Her early constitution had been aristocratic, and its form had not really changed. For many years there had been constant friction between the *optimates* (the 'noble' families) and the *populares*, or democratic party. One leader after another had risen, tried to alter matters in one way or other, and failed.

Inside Italy too there was constant economic trouble, constant difficulty with agriculture, and a constant and unhealthy flow from the countryside to Rome. These troubles were accentuated after 133–122 B.C., when the brothers Gaius and Tiberius Sempronius Gracchus with their reforms first seriously challenged the supremacy of the Senate. Fresh shocks came in Caesar's own time. In 91–89 B.C., the disgruntled 'allied' peoples of

Italy took up arms, and were pacified by the grant of citizenship. There was bloody civil war in 88 B.C. and again in 83–82 B.C., between the *populares* under Caesar's uncle by marriage, G. Marius, and later under Gnaeus Papirius Carbo and Lucius Cornelius Cinna, and the *optimates*, led by the great L. Cornelius Sulla. Sulla was victorious, but there followed one crisis after another. There was the rising of the slaves, under Spartacus and Crixus, in 73–1 B.C. Individualists arose like Gnaeus Pompeius Magnus the soldier, and Marcus Licinius Crassus the banker. Lucius Sergius Catilina tried to introduce startling reforms, first by standing as consul, then by conspiracy and violence. More peaceful characters like the great orator Marcus Tullius Cicero, who pleaded for peace and harmony, and Marcus Porcius Cato, the upholder of tradition, were swept aside. Things could not go on in this way, and it was to be Caesar who irretrievably changed the old order.

III. CAESAR

Gaius Julius Caesar was born between 102 and 100 B.C.; the date is not certain. He was of distinguished family, and traced his descent from royalty and even from the gods. His aunt Julia married the great soldier and democratic leader Gaius Marius. Whilst still a boy, Caesar was named as *Flamen Dialis*, the second of the great priests of Rome, and married Cornelia, daughter of Cinna, the democratic leader. He was associated with the popular party, but escaped the reign of terror which followed the victory of Sulla over the democrats and the restoration of the power to the aristocrats in 82 B.C.

His early career did not have the spectacular early successes of his later colleague and rival, Pompey ' the Great.' He served as aide-de-camp (*contubernalis*) in Bithynia, in Asia Minor; returned to Rome, and became famous as an orator. He again saw service in

Asia (74 B.C.) where he seems to have taken some responsibility for a time. He was elected military tribune in 73 B.C., but it was to be a long time before he again won distinction in war. He pursued the normal course of honours. In 68 B.C. he served as quaestor in Further Spain. It is said that he became restless, and returned to Rome before finishing his tour of duty. In 65 B.C. he was aedile, or commissioner of works, and spent vast sums on public buildings and games for the populace. He ran heavily into debt, and became deeply obliged to the great banker M. Licinius Crassus. He was almost certainly associated with L. Sergius Catilina, who in the years before 63 B.C. tried by every legal and illegal means to seize the chief power; he was not involved in Catilina's downfall, though he spoke strongly against the conspirators' execution, and almost succeeded in saving their lives. The years of waiting were drawing to their close. In 63 B.C. he was elected Pontifex Maximus, or Chief Priest; in 62 he was Praetor, the second of the great officers of state; and in 61–60 he governed Further Spain as propraetor. He administered the province well, and carried out a successful campaign in the west.

He returned to Rome in 60 B.C. anxious for the consulship and for a proconsular command. To gain these, he needed support. The Senate was now secure in its authority, and the more conservative members, such as Cato, held the upper hand. Two others besides Caesar, and of more note than Caesar, needed help to gain their ends—Pompey and Crassus. Pompey had lately returned from brilliant campaigns against the pirates who had overrun the Mediterranean, and against Mithridates, King of Pontus, and had thoroughly reorganised the Middle East. The Senate, however, had refused to ratify his acts or pension his troops. Crassus had been refused permission to readjust some large financial deals in the East, and was anxious besides about Caesar's ability to pay his debts to him. With Pompey and Crassus, therefore, Caesar formed the coalition known as the First Triumvirate. Although at the time, in achievement and prestige, he was the 'junior partner,' he was the driving-force behind the alliance. He cemented the alliance by marrying to Pompey his daughter Julia. He tried to induce the orator Cicero to join them, but Cicero refused.

With the backing of Pompey and Crassus, Caesar became consul for 59 B.C. Despite obstruction from his senatorial colleague M. Bibulus, and an attempt to side-track him into a trivial proconsular command, he obtained the governorship of Cisalpine Gaul and Illyricum, and to this was almost at once added Transalpine Gaul, on the death of its governor-elect. He took up this command in 58 B.C., and from then onwards speaks for himself in his Commentaries.

The rest of his story can be briefly told. Until his death in 44 B.C., only one year (50 B.C.) was not occupied in travelling and fighting, and that year was full of anxious political struggle. He subdued Gaul; taught aggressive Germans a bitter lesson; twice invaded Britain; and kept always a clear eye on the dangerous and murky political situation at Rome. He had capable subordinates, but he was throughout the controller and mainspring of action, and established progressively his ascendancy over men's minds as over his enemies in the field. When Gaul was pacified, and his command drew to a close, he was forced by his political opponents into civil war against the Senate and against Pompey, from whom he had become estranged. The leaders of the senatorial party entrenched themselves all over the Empire, save only in Gaul. Everywhere Caesar went, and everywhere he conquered; in Spain, in Greece, in Egypt, in Asia Minor, in Africa, and last of all (once more) in Spain. Between and after these campaigns, he carried out a thousand reforms, and planned an expedition to the East, where the warlike Parthians had beaten and killed Crassus, and threatened the Roman power. He was the first man in the world. He had grown too great. A group of jealous men, led by an idealist, M. Junius Brutus, conspired and killed him in the senate house, at the foot of Pompey's statue, on March 15th, 44 B.C.

His character was many-sided and dominating. He was a great orator, a great writer, a great politician, and a great statesman. Though constant wars, and his premature death, curtailed his work in the latter capacity, he achieved an astonishing amount, which shows how much more he might have done. He was, by the standards of his time, no mean scientist, and his reform of the calendar has lasted, with adjustments, till today. He was one of the great generals of all time, supreme as strategist and tactician. He had outstanding personal courage, and uncanny powers of leadership and managing men. He could be ruthless if it was necessary to teach a lesson (see his treatment of the Helvetians in Book I, ch. xxviii). On the other hand, his mercy in other ways became proverbial. He had the great man's power of taking decisions suitable for the occasion, of carrying them through, and of taking responsibility for them.

What were the results of his work ? He made Gaul Roman, once for all, and prevented the German peoples from extending their sway to the Atlantic. He ended the old, outworn form of Roman government. Though he could not finish the work, and though after his death there still remained fourteen years of civil war, his legacy and example made it possible for his great-nephew and adopted son, C. Octavius—later the Emperor Augustus—to consolidate, strengthen, and organise the Empire as a whole. His name became legendary, and lasted till our own times in the titles of Kings and Emperors.

IV. The Composition, Purpose, and Reliability of the Commentaries

Caesar had no clear idea that he was going to conquer Gaul. He received the Transalpine province at the last moment. At the beginning of his term of office, most of his army was stationed at Aquileia, on the Illyrian side of his command, to meet a possible danger from the Dacians of Roumania. After the first campaigns, in 58 B.C., he left his army in winter-quarters in Sequanian territory in central Gaul, and thenceforward the conquest developed step by step.

He was as methodical as he was successful. At all times he must have kept a full record of his operations— by means of despatches and reports from his officers; of notes and documents prepared by his secretaries; of diaries kept by himself; and of copies of his regular reports to the Senate. It is not certain when he wrote the Commentaries themselves, but two suggestions have been made. One is that he spent part of each winter during his command in setting down a full account of the previous year's campaigning, but refrained from publishing them until the winter of 51–50 B.C.; the other that he composed the whole work at once, soon after the end of Vercingetorix' revolt in 52 B.C. Even if the Commentaries were composed year by year, it seems unlikely that they were also published annually, as some have suggested. Cicero does not mention them till much later, though he was writing throughout the period. Aulus Hirtius, who continued Caesar's narrative in Book VIII, describing the operations of 51 and 50 B.C., said after Caesar's death, ' *contexui* '—' I put them together.' This may mean ' edited for first publication ' (doubtless in 51–50 B.C.) or ' revised for a second edition ' later on.

We may assume, then, that the Commentaries were published all together, probably in 51–50 B.C., being put together either by Caesar himself, or by Hirtius, and possibly revised later by Hirtius.

Caesar's purpose in writing was (in Hirtius' words) ' to provide material for future historians.' Towards the end of his command, it became important also to tell his own contemporaries what had been done, and to do so without delay. The Gallic war was finished. He had many foes at Rome. His coalition had broken up; Crassus was dead, Julia was dead, and Pompey was drifting to the opposite side. Caesar's command in Gaul would end in early 49 B.C. When he returned, he might face trial for misconduct, and ruin. He wished to tell his story, clearly and finally, and to set down all that he had done. It is hard, though, to think that he had not two other reasons for writing: first, the artist's pleasure in the completion of a great work—both as a soldier and as a writer; second, the wish himself to tell his tale to future generations. As Hirtius said, Caesar did not so much provide material for others as do their work for them.

His style is powerful, lucid and brief. Though he was trained in rhetoric, and though flowing language and exaggeration were the fashion, he quietly let the facts speak for themselves. His ' simplicity ' is that of complete mastery of language and material. His arrangement of his facts, and his emphasis, are masterly; he is never laboured or involved. Blemishes there are, but they are rare. He writes in the third person, always calling himself ' Caesar '; he very rarely lets his personal feelings show. Sometimes—for example in Chapters xl and xlii of Book I—there is a delicious touch of humour, most gravely inserted.

He has often been attacked, as has every great man. He has been accused of suppressing facts, of falsifying the truth, and of mis-stating his own motives. Many of these charges can be shown to be almost certainly false. Three examples can be given.

(1) He describes, in Chapter xii, the rout of the Tigurini as carried out by himself. Later historians, including the Greek Plutarch (nearly 150 years later), say it was done by Labienus, and some modern scholars follow this story. But there is no contemporary evidence for this, and such a lie would surely not in his own time have gone unchallenged.

(2) It is alleged that Caesar's account of his parley with Ariovistus (chs. xliii–xlvi) is one-sided and biased. One-sided it must be, since Caesar spoke through interpreters; but, on a careful reading, both the arguments (in general) and the events seem in every way probable. Even Ariovistus's astonishing offer to ' do any fighting Caesar wished,' if Caesar would give him a free hand, has been heard in our own time, when in 1939 Hitler offered to ' guarantee the British Empire,' if the British would not ' interfere ' in Europe.

(3) It has been said that Caesar wantonly exaggerated the numbers of his enemies—e.g., in the Helvetian migration (ch. xxix). How, it is asked, could 368,000 souls be reduced in so short a time to 110,000? The answer is easy; Caesar did not say that 368,000 actually migrated. He says that the Helvetian lists gave this figure; he says clearly that the census of those who returned gave the figure of 110,000. No doubt many never marched; many others scattered, or died on the way; wagons would break down, and be abandoned; perhaps the Helvetian figures were inaccurate.

There is even negative evidence in Caesar's favour; at the crisis of the battle with Ariovistus, Caesar rightly gives ' young Publius Crassus ' the credit of turning the tide, and unintentionally shows that he himself was so involved in the fighting elsewhere that he had at the moment no control at the keypoint of the battle.

No doubt in some places Caesar does omit facts, or interpret them in the light of his own knowledge, intention, or future policy. A man's account of events must be coloured by the fact that he took part in them, controlled them by his decisions and actions, and must try to explain them to those who may judge and blame, but did not carry the responsibility.

The question of his motives for various actions can be illustrated by two very important statements of policy in Book I. In ch. x, he says that he did not wish a warlike and hostile people (the Helvetii) to become neighbours to the most exposed and richest parts of the Province. Again in ch. xxviii, he says that he ordered the beaten invaders to return home, to fill the void they would otherwise have left, which would have tempted the Germans to move south and west, to the danger of the Province, and to the temptation of the restless Allobroges. Both of these motives appear more than sensible, and need no justification. Whatever his personal motives, he was carrying out his public duty, which was to maintain a settled and progressive civilisation against nomadic and semi-barbaric peoples, who had for centuries moved restlessly to and fro, and were to continue to do so until, centuries later, they brought down the Roman Empire.

It has been said that Caesar is careless in matters of geography. Now he could scarcely in such matters give the detail of Strabo or Pausanias, professional geographers in whose works difficulties nevertheless arise. The fact is that no soldier, and no geographer, can always be precise unless he can refer to accurate maps; and such maps simply did not then exist, nor for many centuries to come. Other marks of identification—exact place-names of known localities, and well-established roads of known length—were likewise in many cases lacking; Gaul was a big country, sparsely provided with big towns, and not yet covered with a network of Roman roads. In spite of all this, Caesar's words often make possible exact identification of obscure sites. Generally, however, without maps, without roads, and without known place-names, it is hard to see how a commander operating often for the first time, in scarcely known country, could have been much more exact than was Caesar.

V. GAUL

It is best to treat Gaul (as did Caesar) as the area of Western Europe which is bounded, on the East, by the Rhine and the Alps; on the South, by the Pyrenees; and elsewhere, by the sea.

From earliest times, the peoples of northern and central Europe were given to migration, in the search for a better and easier way of life. In general, these peoples were Nordic—from Scandinavia and Germany —and 'Celtic,' from central Europe. In the sixth century B.C., the Celts moved south and west, under pressure from Nordic invaders. Particularly, they entered Gaul, hitherto inhabited by Ligurians (in the south-east and centre) and Iberians (in the west). In the south-west—Aquitania—they mingled with the original Iberian (Spanish) inhabitants; elsewhere, and especially in central Gaul, they became dominant.

Some of them stayed east of the Rhine, joined the Nordic invaders, and—in the second century B.C.— crossed into Belgium. This gives Caesar's three divisions (ch. i), of Gallia Celtica, Gallia Belgica, and Aquitania.

The 'Gauls' were different from the Germans, and they found Gaul to their-liking. They ceased to be nomadic, and tribes became settled in different parts of the country. As was natural, the local influences had their effect, so that in Aquitania, Central Gaul, and Belgium, the language, customs, and way of life generally came to differ (ch. i). There was, however, much resemblance, and it is right to regard Gaul, as did Caesar, as 'one whole,'—geographically and ethnographically.

The Celts were first divided into *pagi* which may be

translated 'cantons' or 'clans.' As time went on, and particularly as the peoples became more settled, the clans joined in larger unions which Caesar calls *civitates* —'tribes,' or 'peoples.' The different tribes were independent of each other, and even the small 'clans' had some degree of self-government. Each tribe had its own council (Caesar calls them *senates*—'councils of elders'), and, at one time, there were kings. In Caesar's time, the kings were mostly gone, and in their place were annually-elected magistrates, like the Vergobrets of the Aedui, or perhaps the council kept the power itself. Generally there was anxiety to prevent one man becoming too powerful; in consequence there was no strong guiding authority, and the nobles, supported by retainers, serfs, and bondmen, were constantly intriguing to seize the supreme power.

The same conditions existed between the great tribes. They were in a state of constant rivalry; there were leagues and societies, but they easily fell apart. There was too much individualism, and though the Gauls were proud of their country and of their achievements, they could not unite or maintain a settled common policy or effort.

The civilisation of the Gauls was in many ways advanced, and lacked only the cement of sound political institutions. Their art, particularly in the field of metal-work and enamels, was excellent. The sculptured warriors found at Entremont, the Gallic settlement that preceded Aquae Sextiae in the Province, are truly remarkable. Their clothing, which included breeches —*bracae*, hence *Gallia Bracata* (the nickname given to the Province)—and plaids, could be very good. Ornaments, weapons, pottery and personal belongings were of a high standard. Many such objects we possess in our museums. Large towns there were, well-built and fortified. There were many villages. Their houses were of timber and wattle, and well-thatched. They cultivated their fields well, though wine, and other luxuries, such (in Caesar's words) as tend to ' make men less warlike,' were imported. They mined for minerals. They understood trade and sea-faring, and built ships well capable of resisting the Atlantic gales. The upper classes even cultivated literature and the arts, which they knew from Greek influences—Massilia (Marseilles) was a long-established Greek ' colony '—as well as from contacts with Rome. Thus when Diviciacus came to Rome, he could talk with Cicero. They used coins, first copied from Greek models, which came through Massilia, then from Roman currency; finally they evolved their own.

The religion of the Gauls was Druidism. It was shared by the whole Celtic people, and was the strongest unifying influence. Caesar's description of it in Book VI, ch. xiii–xiv, is the only contemporary account. He says that Druidism originated in Britain, and that Britain was in his day still its home and stronghold. The Druids had vast power, and acted as judges. Their decision was law, and any who refused to accept it were excommunicated and became outcasts. There was a chief Druid. A great synod or council was held each year, at a fixed season, in the country of the Carnutes, near Orléans. The Druids took no part in war, and paid no taxes. Membership of the order was eagerly sought; some remained as long as twenty years studying to enter it. The chief belief was that the soul, on death, passed at once to another body, and there were many other articles of faith connected with the nature of the universe and the power of the gods. Many of their beliefs, however, Caesar calls *religiones*, which to the Romans meant ' superstition '; and the darker side of their religion was marked by human sacrifice conducted by the Druids.

In warfare, they had numerous infantry, but the strongest part of their army was the cavalry. They no longer used chariots. The common soldiers wore no armour, though the chiefs were well equipped. They were far behind the Romans in the understanding of tactics and reconnaissance, in fortification and engineering, and in scientific warfare generally, though they were quick to learn. Mostly they relied on the furious charge and the ambush. They lacked staying-power, and were prone to sudden panic. Discipline was not good, and armies easily melted away; and the political weaknesses mentioned above did not help. But in personal bravery and very often in devotion—to a chief or to their tribe —they showed great qualities.

VI. How the Romans Entered Gaul

Rome became interested in Southern Gaul in the second century B.C. Massilia asked her help against the neighbouring tribes, and this help was granted. Finally in a series of campaigns, between 125–101 B.C., the different tribes were beaten one after the other; Massilia was strengthened and her territory extended; an outpost was established at Aquae Sextiae (Aix-en-Provence); and in 122 and 121, crushing victories over the Allobroges, Arverni and Ruteni, led to the establishment of the province of Transalpine Gaul, called Gallia Narbonensis—from Narbo, a colony planted on the new military road to the Pyrenees,—or simply *provincia*.

A great danger threatened almost at once. Two powerful Nordic or German tribes, the Cimbri and Teutones, were in migration. In 113 they beat the consul Gnaeus Papirius Carbo, on the north-east frontiers of Italy. They moved west, being joined by the Tigurini (a ' canton ' of the Helvetii of Switzerland), and between 109 and 101 gravely threatened the whole of the Roman position in the north. In 107, the Tigurini defeated and killed the consul L. Cassius Longinus (the *bellum Cassianum* is several times mentioned in Book I), and in 105, two Roman armies were routed.

Finally in 102–1 the invaders made for Italy itself and the danger was removed by Marius in two pitched battles, at Aquae Sextiae and the Raudine Plains.

VII. THE ROMAN ARMY

The earliest Roman armies were of citizens, called out in time of need, and the 'levy' or 'gathering' (*legio*)

CENTURIES

		1	2	3	4	5	6
	I	*Primus Pilus*	*Pilus Posterior*	*Princeps Prior*	*Princeps Posterior*	*Hastatus Prior*	*Hastatus Posterior*
	II	*Pilus Prior*	,,	,,	,,	,,	,,
	III	,,	,,	,,	,,	,,	,,
	IV	,,	,,	,,	,,	,,	,,
	V	,,	,,	,,	,,	,,	,,
	VI	,,	,,	,,	,,	,,	,,
	VII	,,	,,	,,	,,	,,	,,
	VIII	,,	,,	,,	,,	,,	,,
	IX	,,	,,	,,	,,	,,	,,
	X	,,	,,	,,	,,	,,	,,
		1		2		3	

COHORTS

MANIPLES

Diagram illustrating the organisation of a legion. The names indicate the ranks of the centurions.

gave its name to the most important military formation, the legion. In Caesar's day, the legions were numbered, and in some cases named. They contained each ten cohorts; each cohort had three maniples, and each maniple, two centuries. At full strength, the legion might contain 6000 men, but generally fell below this figure, and was often much weaker. This organisation was always maintained. The usual battle-formation was the *triplex acies* (see ch. xxiv), with four cohorts in the front line, three in each of the other two. A double or single line was also used when suitable.

The century was the disciplinary unit. It was commanded by a centurion. The centurions were the backbone of the army. They were men of long service, who had risen from the ranks. They maintained strict discipline, and had the power of flogging. There was apparently a regular system of promotion : first, within the cohort, from the sixth to the first century; then, from the tenth to the first cohort. The senior centurion of the legion, *centuro primi pili* or *primipilus*, was a great man indeed.

Each legion had its *aquila*, its 'eagle'; this was a silver eagle, with other adornments, on a long pole, carried by the *aquilifer* or standard-bearer, who wore the skin of some beast over his armour. This emblem was sacred, and it was the greatest disgrace to lose it. There were also subordinate standards, the *signa*, apparently used as badges for the maniples, as rallying-points in battle—so that proper formation could be kept—and to mark the lines in camp.

The commander in war was normally the proconsul or propraetor, and he might 'delegate' the command of a legion to a *legatus*, or deputy—appointed by the Senate, or by the commander himself—who might at times even operate away from his commander. The *tribuni militum*—of whom there were six to a legion—were in Caesar's time generally young men of distinguished family, gaining experience for their future careers. Various duties might be given them, but from ch. xxxix, it seems that Caesar did not hold them in much regard. It was on the commander and on the centurions that most depended, though Caesar was lucky in having such able ' deputies ' as Labienus and others.

Besides the regular infantry, there were *alarii* or *auxilia*—contingents furnished by the allies, who fought on the *alae* (wings), and were in number about one-tenth of the legionaries. The cavalry, too, was provided by the allies—generally Gauls, though German cavalry were also used in Caesar's later campaigns.

The equipment of the infantrymen (*legionarius*) is shown in plate II. Besides his armour and weapons, his kit—rations of grain, entrenching and other tools, cooking-pots, and other personal affairs—his *sarcina* (see ch. xxiv) might weigh in all little less than 100 lb. Carrying this, he would march up to twenty miles in the day—more on a forced march—and, at the end, help as a matter of course to make the properly defended camp, with ditch, mound, and palisade. His labour might be needed to build a bridge or a road, a camp or a fort, and nothing came amiss to him. His courage, discipline, and endurance were unbreakable. His devotion was owed to his centurion, to his legion, and above all to his commander. Through his commander he came, during the last century of the Republic, to control the Roman state.

CAESAR'S GALLIC WAR
BOOK I

NOTE

THE first book of the Commentaries deals with two main subjects: (A) chs. I–XXIX: an account of Gaul, and of the Helvetians' intention to migrate; their march, and their defeat by Caesar near the Rhône. (B) chs. XXX–LIV: the threat to Gaul by the Germans, led by Ariovistus; Caesar's march to meet him, their fruitless negotiations, and the rout of the Germans.

(A) THE MARCH AND DEFEAT OF THE HELVETIANS

CH. I. *A short account of Gaul: its division into three distinct parts.*

I

Gallia est omnis divisa in partis tris, quarum unam incolunt Belgae, aliam Aquitani, tertiam qui ipsorum lingua Celtae, nostra Galli appellantur. Hi omnes lingua, institutis, legibus inter se differunt. Gallos ab Aquitanis Garumna flumen, a Belgis Matrona et Sequana dividit. 5 Horum omnium fortissimi sunt Belgae, propterea quod a cultu atque humanitate provinciae longissime absunt, minimeque ad eos mercatores saepe commeant atque ea quae ad effeminandos animos pertinent important, proximique sunt Germanis qui trans Rhenum incolunt, 10 quibuscum continenter bellum gerunt. Qua de causa Helvetii quoque reliquos Gallos virtute praecedunt, quod fere cotidianis proeliis cum Germanis contendunt, cum aut suis finibus eos prohibent aut ipsi in eorum finibus bellum gerunt. Eorum una pars, quam Gallos obtinere 15 dictum est, initium capit a flumine Rhodano; continetur Garumna flumine, Oceano, finibus Belgarum; attingit etiam ab Sequanis et Helvetiis flumen Rhenum; vergit ad septentriones. Belgae ab extremis Galliae finibus oriuntur; pertinent ad inferiorem partem fluminis Rheni; 20 spectant in septentrionem et orientem solem. Aquitania a Garumna flumine ad Pyrenaeos montis et eam partem Oceani quae est ad Hispaniam pertinet; spectat inter occasum solis et septentriones.

CHS. 2–4. *The Helvetians: their reasons for migrating. The ambition and the conspiracy of Orgetorix: his intrigues with Casticus the Sequanian and Dumnorix the Aeduan. The detection of his plots; his uncompleted trial; his death.*

II

Apud Helvetios longe nobilissimus fuit et ditissimus Orgetorix. Is, M. Messalla et M. Pupio Pisone consulibus, regni cupiditate inductus coniurationem nobilitatis fecit, et civitati persuasit ut de finibus suis cum omnibus copiis
5 exirent: perfacile esse, cum virtute omnibus praestarent, totius Galliae imperio potiri. Id hoc facilius eis persuasit, quod undique loci natura Helvetii continentur: una ex parte flumine Rheno latissimo atque altissimo, qui agrum Helvetium a Germanis dividit; altera ex parte monte Iura
10 altissimo, qui est inter Sequanos et Helvetios; tertia lacu Lemanno et flumine Rhodano, qui provinciam nostram ab Helvetiis dividit. His rebus fiebat ut et minus late vagarentur et minus facile finitimis bellum inferre possent : qua ex parte homines bellandi cupidi magno dolore
15 adficiebantur. Pro multitudine autem hominum et pro gloria belli atque fortitudinis angustos se finis habere arbitrabantur, qui in longitudinem milia passuum CCXL, in latitudinem CLXXX patebant.

III

His rebus adducti et auctoritate Orgetorigis permoti, constituerunt ea quae ad proficiscendum pertinerent comparare, iumentorum et carrorum quam maximum numerum coemere, sementis quam maximas facere ut in
5 itinere copia frumenti suppeteret, cum proximis civitatibus pacem et amicitiam confirmare. Ad eas res con-

ficiendas biennium sibi satis esse duxerunt : in tertium
annum profectionem lege confirmant. Ad eas res
conficiendas Orgetorix deligitur. Is sibi legationem ad
civitates suscepit. In eo itinere persuadet Castico 10
Catamantaloedis filio Sequano, cuius pater regnum in
Sequanis multos annos obtinuerat et a senatu populi
Romani amicus appellatus erat, ut regnum in civitate sua
occuparet quod pater ante habuerat; itemque Dumnorigi
Aeduo fratri Diviciaci, qui eo tempore principatum in 15
civitate obtinebat ac maxime plebi acceptus erat, ut idem
conaretur persuadet, eique filiam suam in matrimonium
dat. Perfacile factu esse illis probat conata perficere,
propterea quod ipse suae civitatis imperium obtenturus
esset : non esse dubium quin totius Galliae plurimum 20
Helvetii possent; se suis copiis suoque exercitu illis regna
conciliaturum confirmat. Hac oratione adducti inter se
fidem et ius iurandum dant, et regno occupato per tris
potentissimos ac firmissimos populos totius Galliae sese
potiri posse sperant.   25

IV

Ea res est Helvetiis per indicium enuntiata. Moribus
suis Orgetorigem ex vinclis causam dicere coegerunt.
Damnatum poenam sequi oportebat ut igni cremaretur.
Die constituta causae dictionis Orgetorix ad iudicium
omnem suam familiam ad hominum milia decem undique 5
coegit, et omnis clientis obaeratosque suos, quorum
magnum numerum habebat, eodem conduxit : per eos ne
causam diceret se eripuit. Cum civitas ob eam rem
incitata armis ius suum exsequi conaretur, multitudinem-
que hominum ex agris magistratus cogerent, Orgetorix 10
mortuus est; neque abest suspicio, ut Helvetii arbitran-
tur, quin ipse sibi mortem consciverit.

CHS. 5–6. *The Helvetians continue their preparations to migrate; the two routes open to them.*

V

Post eius mortem nihilo minus Helvetii id quod constituerant facere conantur, ut e finibus suis exeant. Ubi iam se ad eam rem paratos esse arbitrati sunt, oppida sua omnia, numero ad duodecim, vicos ad quadringentos, 5 reliqua privata aedificia incendunt; frumentum omne, praeterquam quod secum portaturi erant, comburunt, ut domum reditionis spe sublata paratiores ad omnia pericula subeunda essent; trium mensum molita cibaria sibi quemque domo efferre iubent. Persuadent Rauricis 10 et Tulingis et Latovicis finitimis suis uti eodem usi consilio, oppidis suis vicisque exustis, una cum eis proficiscantur, Boiosque, qui trans Rhenum incoluerant et in agrum Noricum transierant Noreiamque oppugnarant, receptos ad se socios sibi asciscunt.

VI

Erant omnino itinera duo, quibus itineribus domo exire possent : unum per Sequanos, angustum et difficile, inter montem Iuram et flumen Rhodanum, vix qua singuli carri ducerentur; mons autem altissimus im- 5 pendebat, ut facile perpauci prohibere possent : alterum per provinciam nostram, multo facilius atque expeditius, propterea quod inter finis Helvetiorum et Allobrogum, qui nuper pacati erant, Rhodanus fluit, isque non nullis locis vado transitur. Extremum oppidum Allobrogum 10 est proximumque Helvetiorum finibus Genava. Ex eo oppido pons ad Helvetios pertinet. Allobrogibus sese vel persuasuros, quod nondum bono animo in populum

Romanum viderentur, existimabant vel vi coacturos ut
per suos finis eos ire paterentur. Omnibus rebus ad
profectionem comparatis, diem dicunt, qua die ad 15
ripam Rhodani omnes conveniant. Is dies erat a. d. V.
Kal. April., L. Pisone A. Gabinio consulibus.

CHS. 7–8. *Caesar hears of their imminent departure;
hastens to Geneva, stops them, and parleys with their
chiefs. They ask for permission to pass through the Roman
province; remembering the wars of fifty years before,
Caesar puts them off. He uses the time gained to strengthen
his fortifications, and refuses to let them pass. They try
to force a passage, but fail.*

VII

Caesari cum id nuntiatum esset, eos per provinciam
nostram iter facere conari, maturat ab urbe proficisci, et
quam maximis potest itineribus in Galliam ulteriorem
contendit, et ad Genavam pervenit. Provinciae toti quam
maximum potest militum numerum imperat (erat omnino 5
in Gallia ulteriore legio una), pontem qui erat ad
Genavam iubet rescindi. Ubi de eius adventu Helvetii
certiores facti sunt, legatos ad eum mittunt nobilissimos
civitatis, cuius legationis Nammeius et Verucloetius
principem locum obtinebant, qui dicerent sibi esse in 10
animo sine ullo maleficio iter per provinciam facere,
propterea quod aliud iter haberent nullum : rogare ut
eius voluntate id sibi facere liceat. Caesar, quod memoria
tenebat L. Cassium consulem occisum exercitumque
eius ab Helvetiis pulsum et sub iugum missum, con- 15
cedendum non putabat; neque homines inimico animo,

data facultate per provinciam itineris faciendi, temperaturos ab iniuria et maleficio existimabat. Tamen, ut
spatium intercedere posset dum milites quos imperaverat
20 convenirent, legatis respondit diem se ad deliberandum
sumpturum : si quid vellent, ad Id. April. reverterentur.

VIII

Interea ea legione quam secum habebat militibusque
qui ex provincia convenerant a lacu Lemanno, qui in
flumen Rhodanum influit, ad montem Iuram, qui finis
Sequanorum ab Helvetiis dividit, milia passuum decem
5 novem murum in altitudinem pedum sedecim fossamque
perducit. Eo opere perfecto, praesidia disponit, castella
communit, quo facilius, si se invito transire conarentur,
prohibere possit. Ubi ea dies quam constituerat cum
legatis venit et legati ad eum reverterunt, negat se more
10 et exemplo populi Romani posse iter ulli per provinciam
dare et, si vim facere conentur, prohibiturum ostendit.
Helvetii ea spe deiecti, navibus iunctis ratibusque compluribus factis alii vadis Rhodani, qua minima altitudo
fluminis erat, non numquam interdiu, saepius noctu, si
15 perrumpere possent conati, operis munitione et militum
concursu et telis repulsi, hoc conatu destiterunt.

CHS. 9–12. *Using Dumnorix's help, the Helvetians*
persuade the Sequanians to let them go through their
country. Caesar resolves nevertheless to stop the Helvetians,
fearing a threat to the west of the Roman province. He
leaves Labienus near Geneva to watch the Helvetians, and
returns to Aquileia to fetch more troops. He marches
swiftly back, fends off attacks on the way from the mountain-
dwelling tribes in the southern Alps, and crosses the frontier

*of the Province. Overtaking the Tigurini, the rearguard
of the Helvetians, he routs them before they can cross the
Saône.*

IX

Relinquebatur una per Sequanos via, qua Sequanis
invitis propter angustias ire non poterant. His cum sua
sponte persuadere non possent, legatos ad Dumnorigem
Aeduum mittunt, ut eo deprecatore a Sequanis impetrarent. Dumnorix gratia et largitione apud Sequanos 5
plurimum poterat, et Helvetiis erat amicus, quod ex ea
civitate Orgetorigis filiam in matrimonium duxerat et,
cupiditate regni adductus, novis rebus studebat et quam
plurimas civitates suo beneficio habere obstrictas volebat.
Itaque rem suscipit et a Sequanis impetrat ut per finis 10
suos Helvetios ire patiantur, obsidesque uti inter sese
dent perficit : Sequani, ne itinere Helvetios prohibeant;
Helvetii, ut sine maleficio et iniuria transeant.

X

Caesari renuntiatur Helvetiis esse in animo per agrum
Sequanorum et Aeduorum iter in Santonum finis facere,
qui non longe a Tolosatium finibus absunt, quae civitas
est in provincia. Id si fieret, intellegebat magno cum
periculo provinciae futurum ut homines bellicosos, populi 5
Romani inimicos, locis patentibus maximeque frumen-
tariis finitimos haberet. Ob eas causas ei munitioni quam
fecerat T. Labienum legatum praefecit; ipse in Italiam
magnis itineribus contendit, duasque ibi legiones con-
scribit, et tris quae circum Aquileiam hiemabant ex 10
hibernis educit et, qua proximum iter in ulteriorem
Galliam per Alpis erat, cum eis quinque legionibus ire

contendit. Ibi Ceutrones et Graioceli et Caturiges, locis
superioribus occupatis, itinere exercitum prohibere
15 conantur. Compluribus eis proeliis pulsis ab Ocelo, quod
est citerioris provinciae extremum, in finis Vocontiorum
ulterioris provinciae die septimo pervenit; inde in
Allobrogum finis, ab Allobrogibus in Segusiavos
exercitum ducit. Hi sunt extra provinciam trans Rhoda-
20 num primi.

XI

Helvetii iam per angustias et finis Sequanorum suas
copias traduxerant, et in Aeduorum finis pervenerant
eorumque agros populabantur. Aedui, cum se suaque ab
eis defendere non possent, legatos ad Caesarem mittunt
5 rogatum auxilium : ita se omni tempore de populo
Romano meritos esse ut paene in conspectu exercitus
nostri agri vastari, liberi eorum in servitutem abduci,
oppida expugnari non debuerint. Eodem tempore Aedui
Ambarri, necessarii et consanguinei Aeduorum,
10 Caesarem certiorem faciunt sese, depopulatis agris, non
facile ab oppidis vim hostium prohibere. Item Allobroges,
qui trans Rhodanum vicos possessionesque habebant,
fuga se ad Caesarem recipiunt, et demonstrant sibi
praeter agri solum nihil esse reliqui. Quibus rebus
15 adductus Caesar non exspectandum sibi statuit dum,
omnibus fortunis sociorum consumptis, in Santonos
Helvetii pervenirent.

XII

Flumen est Arar, quod per finis Aeduorum et Sequanorum in Rhodanum influit, incredibili lenitate, ita ut oculis
in utram partem fluat iudicari non possit. Id Helvetii

ratibus ac lintribus iunctis transibant. Ubi per exploratores Caesar certior factus est tris iam partis copiarum 5
Helvetios id flumen traduxisse, quartam fere partem citra
flumen Ararim reliquam esse, de tertia vigilia cum
legionibus tribus e castris profectus ad eam partem
pervenit, quae nondum flumen transierat. Eos impeditos
et inopinantis aggressus magnam partem eorum concidit : 10
reliqui sese fugae mandarunt atque in proximas silvas
abdiderunt. Is pagus appellabatur Tigurinus : nam
omnis civitas Helvetia in quattuor pagos divisa est. Hic
pagus unus, cum domo exisset, patrum nostrorum
memoria, L. Cassium consulem interfecerat et eius 15
exercitum sub iugum miserat. Ita sive casu sive consilio
deorum immortalium, quae pars civitatis Helvetiae
insignem calamitatem populo Romano intulerat, ea
princeps poenas persolvit. Qua in re Caesar non solum
publicas sed etiam privatas iniurias ultus est, quod eius 20
soceri L. Pisonis avum, L. Pisonem legatum, Tigurini
eodem proelio quo Cassium interfecerant.

Chs. 13–14. *Parley between Caesar and the Helvetians;
his answer to their offers and threats; the parley broken off.*

XIII

Hoc proelio facto, reliquas copias Helvetiorum ut con-
sequi posset, pontem in Arare faciendum curat atque ita
exercitum traducit. Helvetii repentino eius adventu
commoti, cum id quod ipsi diebus xx aegerrime con-
fecerant, ut flumen transirent, illum uno die fecisse 5
intellegerent, legatos ad eum mittunt; cuius legationis
Divico princeps fuit, qui bello Cassiano dux Helvetiorum
fuerat. Is ita cum Caesare egit : si pacem populus
Romanus cum Helvetiis faceret, in eam partem ituros

10 atque ibi futuros Helvetios ubi eos Caesar constituisset
atque esse voluisset; sin bello persequi perseveraret,
reminisceretur et veteris incommodi populi Romani et
pristinae virtutis Helvetiorum. Quod improviso unum
pagum adortus esset, cum ei qui flumen transissent suis
15 auxilium ferre non possent, ne ob eam rem aut suae
magnopere virtuti tribueret aut ipsos despiceret. Se ita
a patribus maioribusque suis didicisse, ut magis virtute
quam dolo contenderent aut insidiis niterentur. Quare
ne committeret ut is locus ubi constitissent ex calamitate
20 populi Romani et internecione exercitus nomen caperet
aut memoriam proderet.

XIV

His Caesar ita respondit : eo sibi minus dubitationis
dari, quod eas res quas legati Helvetii commemorassent
memoria teneret, atque eo gravius ferre quo minus merito
populi Romani accidissent : qui si alicuius iniuriae sibi
5 conscius fuisset, non fuisse difficile cavere; sed eo deceptum, quod neque commissum a se intellegeret quare
timeret neque sine causa timendum putaret. Quod si
veteris contumeliae oblivisci vellet, num etiam recentium
iniuriarum, quod eo invito iter per provinciam per vim
10 temptassent, quod Aeduos, quod Ambarros, quod Allobrogas vexassent, memoriam deponere posse ? Quod sua
victoria tam insolenter gloriarentur, quodque tam diu se
impune iniurias tulisse admirarentur, eodem pertinere.
Consuesse enim deos immortalis, quo gravius homines ex
15 commutatione rerum doleant, quos pro scelere eorum
ulcisci velint, eis secundiores interdum res et diutur-
niorem impunitatem concedere. Cum ea ita sint, tamen,
si obsides ab eis sibi dentur, uti ea quae polliceantur
facturos intellegat, et si Aeduis de iniuriis quas ipsis

sociisque eorum intulerint, item si Allobrogibus satis- 20
faciant, sese cum eis pacem esse facturum. Divico
respondit : ita Helvetios a maioribus suis institutos esse
uti obsides accipere, non dare, consuerint : eius rei
populum Romanum esse testem. Hoc responso dato
discessit. 25

CHS. 15-20. *Caesar's difficulties; his Gallic cavalry
lose a skirmish; he does not offer battle, but keeps in touch
with the enemy. He runs short of provisions, and the
Aeduans fail to supply what they had promised. Caesar
protests. The Aeduan Vergobret, Liscus, blames certain
of his tribesmen, and tells of anti-Roman feeling; pressed
by Caesar, he privately accuses Dumnorix. Dumnorix's
plots and treachery. Diviciacus, the brother of Dumnorix,
begs Caesar not to punish him too severely. Caesar repri-
mands Dumnorix, and puts him under surveillance.*

XV

Postero die castra ex eo loco movent. Idem facit
Caesar, equitatumque omnem ad numerum quattuor
milium, quem ex omni provincia et Aeduis atque eorum
sociis coactum habebat, praemittit, qui videant quas in
partis hostes iter faciant. Qui, cupidius novissimum 5
agmen insecuti, alieno loco cum equitatu Helvetiorum
proelium committunt; et pauci de nostris cadunt. Quo
proelio sublati Helvetii, quod quingentis equitibus tantam multitudinem equitum propulerant, audacius
subsistere non numquam et novissimo agmine proelio 10
nostros lacessere coeperunt. Caesar suos a proelio
continebat, ac satis habebat in praesentia hostem rapinis
pabulationibus populationibusque prohibere. Ita dies

circiter quindecim iter fecerunt uti inter novissimum
15 hostium agmen et nostrum primum non amplius quinis
aut senis milibus passuum interesset.

XVI

Interim cotidie Caesar Aeduos frumentum quod essent
publice polliciti flagitare. Nam propter frigora, quod
Gallia sub septentrionibus, ut ante dictum est, posita est,
non modo frumenta in agris matura non erant, sed ne
5 pabuli quidem satis magna copia suppetebat : eo autem
frumento quod flumine Arare navibus subvexerat propterea uti minus poterat quod iter ab Arare Helvetii averterant, a quibus discedere nolebat. Diem ex die ducere
Aedui : conferri, comportari, adesse dicere. Ubi se
10 diutius duci intellexit et diem instare, quo die frumentum
militibus metiri oporteret, convocatis eorum principibus
quorum magnam copiam in castris habebat, in his
Diviciaco et Lisco, qui summo magistratui praeerat*
quem Vergobretum appellant Aedui, qui creatur annuus
15 et vitae necisque in suos habet potestatem, graviter eos
accusat quod, cum neque emi neque ex agris sumi possit,†
tam necessario tempore, tam propinquis hostibus, ab eis
non sublevetur; praesertim cum magna ex parte eorum
precibus adductus bellum susceperit, multo etiam gravius
20 quod sit destitutus queritur.

XVII

Tum demum Liscus oratione Caesaris adductus, quod
antea tacuerat proponit : esse non nullos, quorum
auctoritas apud plebem plurimum valeat, qui privatim

---

* *Oxford text* praeerant   † *Oxford text* posset

plus possint quam ipsi magistratus. Hos seditiosa atque improba oratione multitudinem deterrere ne frumentum 5 conferant quod debeant : praestare, si iam principatum Galliae obtinere non possent, Gallorum quam Romanorum imperia perferre, neque dubitare* quin, si Helvetios superaverint Romani, una cum reliqua Gallia Aeduis libertatem sint erepturi. Ab eisdem nostra consilia 10 quaeque in castris gerantur hostibus enuntiari : hos a se coerceri non posse. Quin etiam, quod necessariam rem coactus Caesari enuntiarit, intellegere sese quanto id cum periculo fecerit, et ob eam causam quam diu potuerit tacuisse. 15

XVIII

Caesar hac oratione Lisci Dumnorigem Diviciaci fratrem designari sentiebat; sed, quod pluribus praesentibus eas res iactari nolebat, celeriter concilium dimittit, Liscum retinet. Quaerit ex solo ea quae in conventu dixerat. Dicit liberius atque audacius. Eadem secreto 5 ab aliis quaerit; reperit esse vera : ipsum esse Dumnorigem, summa audacia, magna apud plebem propter liberalitatem gratia, cupidum rerum novarum. Compluris annos portoria reliquaque omnia Aeduorum vectigalia parvo pretio redempta habere, propterea quod illo licente 10 contra liceri audeat nemo. His rebus et suam rem familiarem auxisse et facultates ad largiendum magnas comparasse; magnum numerum equitatus suo sumptu semper alere et circum se habere; neque solum domi sed etiam apud finitimas civitates largiter posse; atque 15 huius potentiae causa matrem in Biturigibus homini illic nobilissimo ac potentissimo collocasse, ipsum ex

---

* *In the Oxford text this word is followed by* [debeant]

Helvetiis uxorem habere, sororem ex matre et propinquas
suas nuptum in alias civitates collocasse. Favere et
20 cupere Helvetiis propter eam adfinitatem, odisse etiam
suo nomine Caesarem et Romanos, quod eorum adventu
potentia eius deminuta et Diviciacus frater in antiquum
locum gratiae atque honoris sit restitutus. Si quid
accidat Romanis, summam in spem per Helvetios regni
25 obtinendi venire : imperio populi Romani non modo
de regno sed etiam de ea quam habeat gratia desperare.
Reperiebat etiam in quaerendo Caesar, quod proelium
equestre adversum paucis ante diebus esset factum,
initium eius fugae factum a Dumnorige atque eius
30 equitibus (nam equitatui quem auxilio Caesari Aedui
miserant Dumnorix praeerat) : eorum fuga reliquum esse
equitatum perterritum.

XIX

Quibus rebus cognitis, cum ad has suspiciones
certissimae res accederent, quod per finis Sequanorum
Helvetios traduxisset, quod obsides inter eos dandos
curasset, quod ea omnia non modo iniussu suo et civitatis
5 sed etiam inscientibus ipsis fecisset, quod a magistratu
Aeduorum accusaretur, satis esse causae arbitrabatur
quare in eum aut ipse animadverteret aut civitatem
animadvertere iuberet. His omnibus rebus unum
repugnabat, quod Diviciaci fratris summum in populum
10 Romanum studium, summam in se voluntatem, egregiam
fidem, iustitiam, temperantiam cognoverat; nam ne eius
supplicio Diviciaci animum offenderet verebatur. Itaque
prius quam quicquam conaretur, Diviciacum ad se
vocari iubet et, cotidianis interpretibus remotis, per
15 C. Valerium Procillum, principem Galliae provinciae,

familiarem suum, cui summam omnium rerum fidem
habebat, cum eo colloquitur : simul commonefacit quae
ipso praesente in concilio Gallorum de Dumnorige sint
dicta, et ostendit quae separatim quisque de eo apud se
dixerit. Petit atque hortatur, ut sine eius offensione 20
animi vel ipse de eo causa cognita statuat, vel civitatem
statuere iubeat.

XX

Diviciacus multis cum lacrimis Caesarem complexus
obsecrare coepit ne quid gravius in fratrem statueret :
scire se illa esse vera, nec quemquam ex eo plus quam se
doloris capere, propterea quod, cum ipse gratia plurimum
domi atque in reliqua Gallia, ille minimum propter 5
adulescentiam posset, per se crevisset ; quibus opibus ac
nervis non solum ad minuendam gratiam sed peane ad
perniciem suam uteretur. Sese tamen et amore fraterno
et existimatione vulgi commoveri. Quod si quid ei a
Caesare gravius accidisset, cum ipse eum locum amicitiae 10
apud eum teneret, neminem existimaturum non sua
voluntate factum; qua ex re futurum uti totius Galliae
animi a se averterentur. Haec cum pluribus verbis flens
a Caesare peteret, Caesar eius dextram prendit ; con-
solatus rogat finem orandi faciat ; tanti eius apud se 15
gratiam esse ostendit uti et rei publicae iniuriam et suum
dolorem eius voluntati ac precibus condonet. Dumnorigem ad se vocat, fratrem adhibet ; quae in eo reprehendat
ostendit, quae ipse intellegat, quae civitas queratur
proponit ; monet ut in reliquum tempus omnis sus- 20
piciones vitet ; praeterita se Diviciaco fratri condonare
dicit. Dumnorigi custodes ponit, ut quae agat, quibuscum loquatur scire possit.

CHS. 21–24. *The Helvetians halt: Caesar hopes to catch them between his own forces and those of Labienus. The scheme fails through faulty reports by P. Considius, and the Helvetians escape.*

XXI

Eodem die ab exploratoribus certior factus hostis sub monte consedisse milia passuum ab ipsius castris octo, qualis esset natura montis et qualis in circuitu ascensus, qui cognoscerent misit. Renuntiatum est facilem esse.
5 De tertia vigilia T. Labienum, legatum pro praetore, cum duabus legionibus et eis ducibus qui iter cognoverant summum iugum montis ascendere iubet; quid sui consili sit ostendit. Ipse de quarta vigilia eodem itinere quo hostes ierant ad eos contendit equitatumque omnem ante
10 se mittit. P. Considius, qui rei militaris peritissimus habebatur et in exercitu L. Sullae et postea in M. Crassi fuerat, cum exploratoribus praemittitur.

XXII

Prima luce, cum summus mons a Labieno* teneretur, ipse ab hostium castris non longius mille et quingentis passibus abesset, neque, ut postea ex captivis comperit, aut ipsius adventus aut Labieni cognitus esset, Considius
5 equo admisso ad eum accurrit, dicit montem quem a Labieno occupari voluerit ab hostibus teneri : id se a Gallicis armis atque insignibus cognovisse. Caesar suas copias in proximum collem subducit, aciem instruit. Labienus, ut erat ei praeceptum a Caesare ne proelium
10 committeret, nisi ipsius copiae prope hostium castra

* *Oxford text* [Lucio] Labieno

visae essent, ut undique uno tempore in hostis impetus fieret, monte occupato nostros exspectabat proelioque abstinebat. Multo denique die per exploratores Caesar cognovit et montem a suis teneri, et Helvetios castra movisse, et Considium timore perterritum quod non 15 vidisset pro viso sibi renuntiasse. Eo die quo consuerat intervallo hostis sequitur, et milia passuum tria ab eorum castris castra ponit.

CHS. 23–26. Short of provisions, Caesar breaks off the pursuit; his movements are betrayed by deserters; the Helvetians turn and begin to attack him. Caesar holds off their first attack, chooses his ground, and prepares for battle. After a long and bitter struggle, the Romans prevail, and the remnant of the Helvetians take to flight. Caesar cannot follow at once, but orders the Lingones not to help them.

XXIII

Postridie eius diei, quod omnino biduum supererat cum exercitui frumentum metiri oporteret, et quod a Bibracte, oppido Aeduorum longe maximo et copiosissimo, non amplius milibus passuum XVIII aberat, rei frumentariae prospiciendum existimavit : iter ab 5 Helvetiis avertit ac Bibracte ire contendit. Ea res per fugitivos L. Aemili, decurionis equitum Gallorum, hostibus nuntiatur. Helvetii, seu quod timore perterritos Romanos discedere a se existimarent, eo magis quod pridie superioribus locis occupatis proelium non com- 10 misissent, sive eo quod re frumentaria intercludi posse confiderent, commutato consilio atque itinere converso nostros a novissimo agmine insequi ac lacessere coeperunt.

XXIV

Postquam id animum advertit, copias :uas Caesar in proximum collem subducit, equitatumque qui sustineret hostium impetum misit. Ipse interim in colle medio triplicem aciem instruxit legionum quattuor veteranorum;*
5 sed in summo iugo duas legiones quas in Gallia citeriore proxime conscripserat et omnia auxilia collocari, ac totum montem hominibus compleri, et interea sarcinas in unum locum conferri, et eum ab eis qui in superiore acie constiterant muniri iussit. Helvetii cum omnibus suis
10 carris secuti impedimenta in unum locum contulerunt; ipsi confertissima acie, reiecto nostro equitatu, phalange facta sub primam nostram aciem successerunt.

XXV

Caesar primum suo, deinde omnium ex conspectu remotis equis, ut aequato omnium periculo spem fugae tolleret, cohortatus suos proelium commisit. Milites e loco superiore pilis missis facile hostium phalangem
5 perfregerunt. Ea disiecta, gladiis destrictis in eos impetum fecerunt. Gallis magno ad pugnam erat impedimento quod pluribus eorum scutis uno ictu pilorum transfixis et colligatis, cum ferrum se inflexisset, neque evellere neque sinistra impedita satis commode
10 pugnare poterant; multi ut diu iactato bracchio praeoptarent scutum manu emittere et nudo corpore pugnare. Tandem vulneribus defessi et pedem referre et, quod mons suberat circiter mille passuum, eo se recipere coeperunt. Capto monte et succedentibus nostris, Boii et
15 Tulingi, qui hominum milibus circiter xv agmen hostium

* *In the Oxford text this word is followed by* [ita uti supra]

claudebant et novissimis praesidio erant, ex itinere nostros latere aperto aggressi circumvenere, et id conspicati Helvetii, qui in montem sese receperant, rursus instare et proelium redintegrare coeperunt. Romani conversa signa bipertito intulerunt: prima et secunda 20 acies, ut victis ac summotis resisteret; tertia, ut venientis sustineret.

XXVI

Ita ancipiti proelio diu atque acriter pugnatum est. Diutius cum sustinere nostrorum impetus non possent, alteri se, ut coeperant, in montem receperunt, alteri ad impedimenta et carros suos se contulerunt. Nam hoc toto proelio, cum ab hora septima ad vesperum pugnatum 5 sit, aversum hostem videre nemo potuit. Ad multam noctem etiam ad impedimenta pugnatum est, propterea quod pro vallo carros obiecerant, et e loco superiore in nostros venientis tela coiciebant, et non nulli inter carros rotasque mataras ac tragulas subiciebant nostrosque 10 vulnerabant. Diu cum esset pugnatum, impedimentis castrisque nostri potiti sunt. Ibi Orgetorigis filia atque unus e filiis captus est. Ex eo proelio circiter hominum milia cxxx superfuerunt, eaque tota nocte continenter ierunt: nullam partem noctis itinere intermisso in finis 15 Lingonum die quarto pervenerunt, cum et propter vulnera militum et propter sepulturam occisorum nostri triduum morati eos sequi non potuissent. Caesar ad Lingonas litteras nuntiosque misit, ne eos frumento neve alia re iuvarent: qui si iuvissent, se eodem loco 20 quo Helvetios habiturum. Ipse triduo intermisso cum omnibus copiis eos sequi coepit.

CHS. 27–29. *The Helvetians surrender. Some of one of their clans try to escape, but are caught and brought back. Not wishing the Helvetians' country to be overrun by the Germans, Caesar orders them to return home, and instructs their neighbours the Allobroges to supply them with provisions. The Boii, who had marched with the Helvetians, are settled in the Aeduan country. An account of the numbers of Helvetians and other tribes who joined the migration.*

XXVII

Helvetii omnium rerum inopia adducti legatos de deditione ad eum miserunt. Qui cum eum in itinere convenissent seque ad pedes proiecissent suppliciterque locuti flentes pacem petissent, atque eos in eo loco quo
5 tum essent suum adventum exspectare iussisset, paruerunt. Eo postquam Caesar pervenit, obsides, arma, servos qui ad eos perfugissent poposcit. Dum ea conquiruntur et conferuntur, nocte intermissa, circiter hominum milia sex eius pagi qui Verbigenus appellatur,
10 sive timore perterriti, ne armis traditis supplicio adficerentur, sive spe salutis inducti, quod in tanta multitudine dediticiorum suam fugam aut occultari aut omnino ignorari posse existimarent, prima nocte e castris Helvetiorum egressi ad Rhenum finisque Germanorum
15 contenderunt.

XXVIII

Quod ubi Caesar resciit, quorum per finis ierant his uti conquirerent et reducerent, si sibi purgati esse vellent,

imperavit : reductos in hostium numero habuit; reliquos
omnis obsidibus, armis, perfugis traditis in deditionem
accepit. Helvetios, Tulingos, Latovicos in finis suos, 5
unde erant profecti, reverti iussit, et, quod omnibus
frugibus amissis domi nihil erat quo famem tolerarent,
Allobrogibus imperavit ut his frumenti copiam facerent :
ipsos oppida vicosque, quos incenderant, restituere iussit.
Id ea maxime ratione fecit, quod noluit eum locum unde 10
Helvetii discesserant vacare, ne propter bonitatem
agrorum Germani qui trans Rhenum incolunt e suis
finibus in Helvetiorum finis transirent et finitimi Galliae
provinciae Allobrogibusque essent. Boios, petentibus
Aeduis, quod egregia virtute erant cogniti, ut in finibus 15
suis collocarent, concessit, quibus illi agros dederunt,
quosque postea in parem iuris libertatisque condicionem
atque ipsi erant receperunt.

XXIX

In castris Helvetiorum tabulae repertae sunt litteris
Graecis confectae, et ad Caesarem relatae, quibus in
tabulis nominatim ratio confecta erat, qui numerus domo
exisset eorum, qui arma ferre possent, et item separatim
pueri, senes mulieresque. Quarum omnium rerum 5
summa erat capitum Helvetiorum milia CCLXIII, Tulingo-
rum milia XXXVI, Latovicorum XIIII, Rauricorum XXIII,
Boiorum XXXII : ex his qui arma ferre possent, ad milia
nonaginta duo. Summa omnium fuerunt ad milia
CCCLXVIII. Eorum qui domum redierunt censu habito, 10
ut Caesar imperaverat, repertus est numerus milium C
et decem.

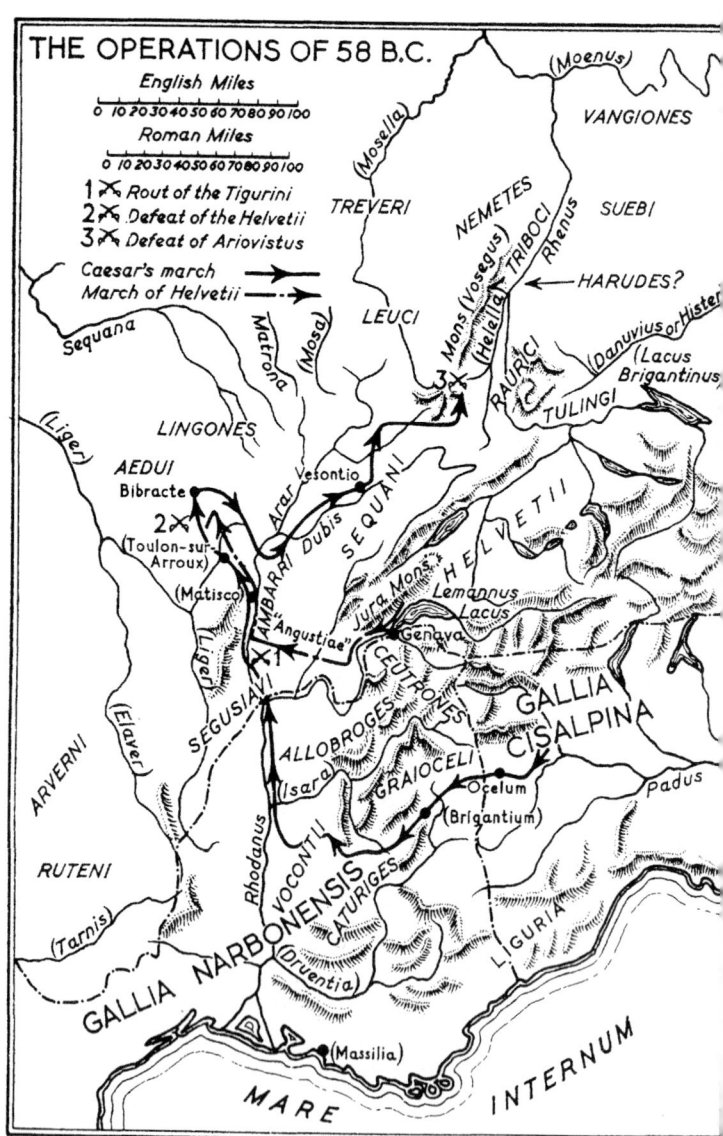

THE OPERATIONS OF 58 B.C.

English Miles
0 10 20 30 40 50 60 70 80 90 100

Roman Miles
0 10 20 30 40 50 60 70 80 90 100

1 ✕ Rout of the Tigurini
2 ✕ Defeat of the Helvetii
3 ✕ Defeat of Ariovistus

Caesar's march ➝
March of Helvetii ➝

(Moenus)

VANGIONES

TREVERI

NEMETES

SUEBI

(Mosella)

Mons (Vosegus)

RAURICI

(Helella) TRIBOCI

Rhenus

HARUDES?

LEUCI

(Danuvius or Hister)

(Lacus Brigantinus)

Sequana

Matrona (Mosa)

TULINGI

(Liger)

LINGONES

Arar

Vesontio

SEQUANI

HELVETII

AEDUI
Bibracte

2 ✕
(Toulon-sur-Arroux)

Dubis

Jura Mons

Lemannus
Lacus

(Matisco)

"AMBARRI"

"Angustiae"

Genava

GALLIA
CISALPINA

Liger

SEGUSIANI

CEUTRONES

(Elaver)

1 ✕

ALLOBROGES

GRAIOCELI

Ocelum

Padus

ARVERNI

(Isara)

VOCONTII

(Brigantium)

RUTENI

CATURIGES

Rhodanus

LIGURIA

(Tarnis)

GALLIA NARBONENSIS

(Druentia)

(Massilia)

MARE

INTERNUM

(B) THE DEFEAT OF ARIOVISTUS AND THE GERMANS

CHS. 30–33. *Many Gallic tribes congratulate Caesar, but ask also for a conference to discuss something else. At a private meeting, certain Gallic chiefs tell him how the Sequanians and Arvernians had first asked the Germans, under Ariovistus, to help them against the Aeduans: how arrogantly and cruelly the Germans were behaving, how more and more of them were entering and settling in Gaul, and how badly the Sequanians had suffered; how the Gauls had taken arms, but had been beaten. To avenge his allies, the Aeduans, and to prevent further danger, Caesar resolves to act.*

XXX

Bello Helvetiorum confecto, totius fere Galliae legati, principes civitatum, ad Caesarem gratulatum convenerunt : intellegere sese, tametsi pro veteribus Helvetiorum iniuriis populi Romani ab his poenas bello repetisset, tamen eam rem non minus ex usu terrae 5 Galliae quam populi Romani accidisse; propterea quod eo consilio florentissimis rebus domos suas Helvetii reliquissent, uti toti Galliae bellum inferrent imperioque potirentur, locumque domicilio ex magna copia deligerent quem ex omni Gallia opportunissimum ac fructuosissi- 10 mum iudicassent, reliquasque civitates stipendiarias habe- rent. Petierunt uti sibi concilium totius Galliae in diem certam indicere idque Caesaris voluntate facere liceret : sese habere quasdam res quas ex communi consensu ab eo petere vellent. Ea re permissa, diem concilio con- 15 stituerunt et iure iurando ne quis enuntiaret, nisi quibus communi consilio mandatum esset, inter se sanxerunt.

XXXI

Eo concilio dimisso, idem principes civitatum qui
ante fuerant ad Caesarem reverterunt, petieruntque uti
sibi secreto* de sua omniumque salute cum eo agere
liceret. Ea re impetrata, sese omnes flentes Caesari
5 ad pedes proiecerunt : non minus se id contendere et
laborare ne ea quae dixissent enuntiarentur, quam uti ea
quae vellent impetrarent; propterea quod, si enuntiatum
esset, summum in cruciatum se venturos viderent.
Locutus est pro his Diviciacus Aeduus : Galliae totius
10 factiones esse duas : harum alterius principatum tenere
Aeduos, alterius Arvernos. Hi cum tantopere de poten-
tatu inter se multos annos contenderent, factum esse uti
ab Arvernis Sequanisque Germani mercede arcesserentur.
Horum primo circiter milia xv Rhenum transisse :
15 posteaquam agros et cultum et copias Gallorum homines
feri ac barbari adamassent, traductos pluris : nunc esse
in Gallia ad centum et viginti milium numerum. Cum
his Aeduos eorumque clientis semel atque iterum armis
contendisse; magnam calamitatem pulsos accepisse,
20 omnem nobilitatem, omnem senatum, omnem equitatum
amisisse. Quibus proeliis calamitatibusque fractos, qui
et sua virtute et populi Romani hospitio atque amicitia
plurimum ante in Gallia potuissent, coactos esse Sequanis
obsides dare nobilissimos civitatis et iure iurando civita-
25 tem obstringere, sese neque obsides repetituros neque
auxilium a populo Romano imploraturos neque recusa-
turos quo minus perpetuo sub illorum dicione atque
imperio essent. Unum se esse ex omni civitate Aeduorum
qui adduci non potuerit ut iuraret aut liberos suos
30 obsides daret. Ob eam rem se ex civitate profugisse et
Romam ad senatum venisse auxilium postulatum, quod

* *In the Oxford text this word is followed by* [in occulto]

solus neque iure iurando neque obsidibus teneretur. Sed peius victoribus Sequanis quam Aeduis victis accidisse, propterea quod Ariovistus, rex Germanorum, in eorum finibus consedisset tertiamque partem agri Sequani, qui 35 esset optimus totius Galliae, occupavisset et nunc de altera parte tertia Sequanos decedere iuberet, propterea quod paucis mensibus ante Harudum milia hominum XXIIII ad eum venissent, quibus locus ac sedes pararentur. Futurum esse paucis annis uti omnes ex Galliae finibus 40 pellerentur atque omnes Germani Rhenum transirent: neque enim conferendum esse Gallicum cum Germanorum agro neque hanc consuetudinem victus cum illa comparandam. Ariovistum autem, ut semel Gallorum copias proelio vicerit, quod proelium factum sit Ad- 45 magetobrigae, superbe et crudeliter imperare, obsides nobilissimi cuiusque liberos poscere, et in eos omnia exempla cruciatusque edere, si qua res non ad nutum aut ad voluntatem eius facta sit. Hominem esse barbarum, iracundum, temerarium: non posse eius imperia diutius 50 sustinere. Nisi quid in Caesare populoque Romano sit auxili, omnibus Gallis idem esse faciendum quod Helvetii fecerint, ut domo emigrent, aliud domicilium, alias sedes remotas a Germanis petant fortunamque quaecumque accidat experiantur. Haec si enuntiata Ariovisto sint, 55 non dubitare quin de omnibus obsidibus qui apud eum sint gravissimum supplicium sumat. Caesarem vel auctoritate sua atque exercitus vel recenti victoria vel nomine populi Romani deterrere posse ne maior multitudo Germanorum Rhenum traducatur, Galliamque 60 omnem ab Ariovisti iniuria posse defendere.

XXXII

Hac oratione ab Diviciaco habita, omnes qui aderant magno fletu auxilium a Caesare petere coeperunt.

Animadvertit Caesar unos ex omnibus Sequanos nihil
earum rerum facere quas ceteri facerent sed tristis capite
5 demisso terram intueri. Eius rei quae causa esset miratus
ex ipsis quaesiit. Nihil Sequani respondere, sed in eadem
tristitia taciti permanere. Cum ab his saepius quaereret
neque ullam omnino vocem exprimere posset, idem
Diviciacus Aeduus respondit : hoc esse miseriorem et
10 graviorem fortunam Sequanorum quam reliquorum,
quod soli ne in occulto quidem queri neque auxilium
implorare auderent absentisque Ariovisti crudelitatem,
velut si coram adesset, horrerent; propterea quod reliquis
tamen fugae facultas daretur, Sequanis vero, qui intra
15 finis suos Ariovistum recepissent, quorum oppida omnia
in potestate eius essent, omnes cruciatus essent perferendi.

XXXIII

His rebus cognitis, Caesar Gallorum animos verbis
confirmavit, pollicitusque est sibi eam rem curae futuram :
magnam se habere spem et beneficio suo et auctoritate
adductum Ariovistum finem iniuriis facturum. Hac
5 oratione habita concilium dimisit. Et secundum ea
multae res eum hortabantur quare sibi eam rem cogitan-
dam et suscipiendam putaret; in primis quod Aeduos,
fratres consanguineosque saepe numero a senatu appellatos, in servitute atque in dicione videbat Germanorum
10 teneri eorumque obsides esse apud Ariovistum ac
Sequanos intellegebat; quod in tanto imperio populi
Romani turpissimum sibi et rei publicae esse arbitrabatur.
Paulatim autem Germanos consuescere Rhenum transire
et in Galliam magnam eorum multitudinem venire
15 populo Romano periculosum videbat. Neque sibi
homines feros ac barbaros temperaturos existimabat quin,
cum omnem Galliam occupavissent, ut ante Cimbri

Teutonique fecissent, in provinciam exirent atque inde in Italiam contenderent, praesertim cum Sequanos a provincia nostra Rhodanus divideret; quibus rebus quam 20 maturrime occurrendum putabat. Ipse autem Ariovistus tantos sibi spiritus, tantam arrogantiam sumpserat ut ferendus non videretur.

Chs. 34–36. *Caesar invites Ariovistus to meet him; Ariovistus haughtily refuses. Caesar again reminds Ariovistus of past services, and asks him to change his policy, making it clear that he was in earnest. Ariovistus refuses point-blank, and tells Caesar not to interfere.*

XXXIV

Quam ob rem placuit ei ut ad Ariovistum legatos mitteret qui ab eo postularent uti aliquem locum medium utriusque colloquio deligeret : velle sese de re publica et summis utriusque rebus cum eo agere. Ei legationi Ariovistus respondit : si quid ipsi a Caesare opus esset, sese ad 5 eum venturum fuisse; si quid ille se velit, illum ad se venire oportere. Praeterea se neque sine exercitu in eas partis Galliae venire audere quas Caesar possideret, neque exercitum sine magno commeatu atque molimento in unum locum contrahere posse. Sibi autem mirum 10 videri quid in sua Gallia quam bello vicisset aut Caesari aut omnino populo Romano negoti esset.

XXXV

His responsis ad Caesarem relatis, iterum ad eum Caesar legatos cum his mandatis mittit : quoniam tanto suo populique Romani beneficio adfectus, cum in consulatu suo rex atque amicus a senatu appellatus esset,

5 hanc sibi populoque Romano gratiam referret ut in colloquium venire invitatus gravaretur neque de communi re dicendum sibi et cognoscendum putaret, haec esse quae ab eo postularet : primum, ne quam multitudinem hominum amplius trans Rhenum in Galliam 10 traduceret; deinde obsides quos haberet ab Aeduis redderet, Sequanisque permitteret ut quos illi haberent voluntate eius reddere illis liceret; neve Aeduos iniuria lacesseret neve his sociisque eorum bellum inferret. Si id ita fecisset, sibi populoque Romano perpetuam gratiam 15 atque amicitiam cum eo futuram : si non impetraret, sese, quoniam M. Messalla M. Pisone consulibus senatus censuisset uti quicumque Galliam provinciam obtineret, quod commodo rei publicae facere posset, Aeduos ceterosque amicos populi Romani defenderet, se Aedu- 20 orum iniurias non neglecturum.

XXXVI

Ad haec Ariovistus respondit : ius esse belli ut qui vicissent eis quos vicissent quem ad modum vellent imperarent : item populum Romanum victis non ad alterius praescriptum sed ad suum arbitrium imperare 5 consuesse. Si ipse populo Romano non praescriberet quem ad modum suo iure uteretur, non oportere sese a populo Romano in suo iure impediri. Aeduos sibi, quoniam belli fortunam temptassent et armis congressi ac superati essent, stipendiarios esse factos. Magnam 10 Caesarem iniuriam facere, qui suo adventu vectigalia sibi deteriora faceret. Aeduis se obsides redditurum non esse, neque his neque eorum sociis iniuria bellum inlaturum, si in eo manerent quod convenisset stipendiumque quotannis penderent : si id non fecissent, longe his 15 fraternum nomen populi Romani afuturum. Quod sibi

Caesar denuntiaret se Aeduorum iniurias non neglecturum, neminem secum sine sua pernicie contendisse.
Cum vellet, congrederetur : intellecturum quid invicti
Germani, exercitatissimi in armis, qui inter annos XIIII
tectum non subissent, virtute possent.   20

CHS. 37–41. *Reports of even more alarming threats of
German invasion. Caesar marches, and occupies the chief
Sequanian town, Vesontio, for which Ariovistus was
reported to be making. A description of the site of Vesontio.
Panic among Caesar's army through terrifying stories of the
Germans. Caesar holds a council of war, makes light of
their fears, tells them to rely on him, and declares that he
will go on even if only the Tenth Legion follow him. The
army recovers its morale. He continues by a roundabout
route and makes contact with Ariovistus.*

XXXVII

Haec eodem tempore Caesari mandata referebantur, et
legati ab Aeduis et a Treveris veniebant : Aedui questum
quod Harudes, qui nuper in Galliam transportati essent,
finis eorum popularentur; sese ne obsidibus quidem datis
pacem Ariovisti redimere potuisse : Treveri autem, pagos   5
centum Sueborum ad ripas Rheni consedisse, qui
Rhenum transire conarentur; his praeesse Nasuam et
Cimberium fratres. Quibus rebus Caesar vehementer
commotus maturandum sibi existimavit, ne, si nova
manus Sueborum cum veteribus copiis Ariovisti sese 10
coniunxisset, minus facile resisti posset. Itaque re
frumentaria quam celerrime potuit comparata, magnis
itineribus ad Ariovistum contendit.

XXXVIII

Cum tridui viam processisset, nuntiatum est ei
Ariovistum cum suis omnibus copiis ad occupandum
Vesontionem, quod est oppidum maximum Sequanorum,
contendere triduique viam a suis finibus profecisse.
5 Id ne accideret, magno opere sibi praecavendum Caesar
existimabat. Namque omnium rerum quae ad bellum
usui erant summa erat in eo oppido facultas; idque natura
loci sic muniebatur ut magnam ad ducendum bellum
daret facultatem, propterea quod flumen Dubis ut
10 circino circumductum paene totum oppidum cingit;
reliquum spatium, quod est non amplius pedum M
sescentorum, qua flumen intermittit, mons continet
magna altitudine, ita ut radices montis ex utraque parte
ripae fluminis contingant. Hunc murus circumdatus
15 arcem efficit et cum oppido coniungit. Huc Caesar
magnis nocturnis diurnisque itineribus contendit,
occupatoque oppido ibi praesidium collocat.

XXXIX

Dum paucos dies ad Vesontionem rei frumentariae
commeatusque causa moratur, ex percontatione nostrorum vocibusque Gallorum ac mercatorum, qui ingenti
magnitudine corporum Germanos, incredibili virtute
5 atque exercitatione in armis esse praedicabant (saepe
numero sese cum his congressos ne vultum quidem atque
aciem oculorum dicebant ferre potuisse), tantus subito
timor omnem exercitum occupavit ut non mediocriter
omnium mentis animosque perturbaret. Hic primum
10 ortus est a tribunis militum, praefectis, reliquisque qui
ex urbe amicitiae causa Caesarem secuti non magnum
in re militari usum habebant; quorum alius alia causa

inlata quam sibi ad proficiscendum necessariam esse
diceret, petebat ut eius voluntate discedere liceret; non
nulli pudore adducti, ut timoris suspicionem vitarent, 15
remanebant. Hi neque vultum fingere neque interdum
lacrimas tenere poterant : abditi in tabernaculis aut suum
fatum querebantur aut cum familiaribus suis commune
periculum miserabantur. Vulgo totis castris testamenta
obsignabantur. Horum vocibus ac timore paulatim 20
etiam ei qui magnum in castris usum habebant, milites
centurionesque quique equitatui praeerant, perturba-
bantur. Qui se ex his minus timidos existimari volebant,
non se hostem vereri sed angustias itineris et magni-
tudinem silvarum quae intercederent inter ipsos atque 25
Ariovistum, aut rem frumentariam, ut satis commode
supportari posset, timere dicebant. Non nulli etiam
Caesari nuntiarant, cum castra moveri ac signa ferri
iussisset, non fore dicto audientis milites neque propter
timorem signa laturos. 30

XL

Haec cum animadvertisset, convocato consilio, omniumque ordinum ad id consilium adhibitis centurionibus, vehementer eos incusavit : primum, quod aut quam
in partem aut quo consilio ducerentur sibi quaerendum
aut cogitandum putarent. Ariovistum, se consule, 5
cupidissime populi Romani amicitiam appetisse : cur
hunc tam temere quisquam ab officio discessurum
iudicaret ? Sibi quidem persuaderi cognitis suis postulatis atque aequitate condicionum perspecta eum neque
suam neque populi Romani gratiam repudiaturum. 10
Quod si furore atque amentia impulsus bellum intulisset,
quid tandem vererentur ? aut cur de sua virtute aut
de ipsius diligentia desperarent ? Factum eius hostis

periculum patrum nostrorum memoria, cum, Cimbris
15 et Teutonis a C. Mario pulsis, non minorem laudem
exercitus quam ipse imperator meritus videbatur; factum
etiam nuper in Italia servili tumultu, quos tamen aliquid
usus ac disciplina quae a nobis accepissent sublevarent.
Ex quo iudicari posse quantum haberet in se boni
20 constantia; propterea quod quos aliquamdiu inermos sine
causa timuissent hos postea armatos ac victores super-
assent. Denique hos esse eosdem quibuscum saepe
numero Helvetii congressi non solum in suis sed etiam
in illorum finibus plerumque superarint, qui tamen
25 pares esse nostro exercitui non potuerint. Si quos
adversum proelium et fuga Gallorum commoveret, hos,
si quaererent, reperire posse diuturnitate belli defati-
gatis Gallis Ariovistum, cum multos mensis castris se ac
paludibus tenuisset neque sui potestatem fecisset,
30 desperantis iam de pugna et dispersos subito adortum
magis ratione et consilio quam virtute vicisse. Cui
rationi contra homines barbaros atque imperitos locus
fuisset, hac ne ipsum quidem sperare nostros exercitus
capi posse. Qui suum timorem in rei frumentariae
35 simulationem angustiasque itineris conferrent, facere
arroganter, cum aut de officio imperatoris desperare aut
praescribere viderentur. Haec sibi esse curae : frumentum Sequanos, Leucos, Lingones sumministrare, iamque
esse in agris frumenta matura; de itinere ipsos brevi
40 tempore iudicaturos. Quod non fore dicto audientes
neque signa laturi dicantur, nihil se ea re commoveri;
scire enim, quibuscumque exercitus dicto audiens non
fuerit, aut male re gesta fortunam defuisse aut aliquo
facinore comperto avaritiam esse convictam : suam
45 innocentiam perpetua vita, felicitatem Helvetiorum bello
esse perspectam. Itaque se quod in longiorem diem

collaturus fuisset repraesentaturum et proxima nocte de
quarta vigilia castra moturum, ut quam primum intellegere posset utrum apud eos pudor atque officium an
timor valeret. Quod si praeterea nemo sequatur, tamen 50
se cum sola decima legione iturum, de qua non dubitaret,
sibique eam praetoriam cohortem futuram. Huic legioni
Caesar et indulserat praecipue et propter virtutem
confidebat maxime.

XLI

Hac oratione habita, mirum in modum conversae sunt
omnium mentes, summaque alacritas et cupiditas belli
gerendi innata est; princepsque decima legio per tribunos
militum ei gratias egit quod de se optimum iudicium
fecisset, seque esse ad bellum gerendum paratissimam 5
confirmavit. Deinde reliquae legiones cum tribunis
militum et primorum ordinum centurionibus egerunt uti
Caesari satisfacerent : se nec umquam dubitasse neque
timuisse neque de summa belli suum iudicium sed
imperatoris esse existimavisse. Eorum satisfactione 10
accepta et itinere exquisito per Diviciacum, quod ex aliis
ei maximam fidem habebat, ut milium amplius quinquaginta circuitu locis apertis exercitum duceret, de
quarta vigilia, ut dixerat, profectus est. Septimo die,
cum iter non intermitteret, ab exploratoribus certior 15
factus est Ariovisti copias a nostris milibus passuum
quattuor et xx abesse.

Chs. 42–46. *Ariovistus offers a parley, but asks that no
infantry shall accompany them. Caesar mounts soldiers of
the Tenth as his bodyguard, instead of the unreliable Gauls.
The parley. Caesar repeats his demands for peace, return
of hostages, and no further encroachment. Ariovistus tells*

*Caesar to mind his own business, says that he intends to
keep the fruits of victory, and tries to buy him off by offering
' to do any fighting he wished,' reminding him of his
enemies at Rome. Caesar repeats his demands. The
Germans grow restless and become threatening; the parley
broken off.*

XLII

Cognito Caesaris adventu, Ariovistus legatos ad eum
mittit : quod antea de colloquio postulasset, id per se fieri
licere, quoniam propius accessisset, seque id sine periculo
facere posse existimare. Non respuit condicionem
5 Caesar, iamque eum ad sanitatem reverti arbitrabatur,
cum id quod antea petenti denegasset ultro polliceretur;
magnamque in spem veniebat pro suis tantis populique
Romani in eum beneficiis, cognitis suis postulatis, fore
uti pertinacia desisteret. Dies colloquio dictus est, ex
10 eo die quintus. Interim saepe ultro citroque cum legati
inter eos mitterentur, Ariovistus postulavit ne quem
peditem ad colloquium Caesar adduceret : vereri se ne
per insidias ab eo circumveniretur : uterque cum
equitatu veniret : alia ratione sese non esse venturum.
15 Caesar, quod neque colloquium interposita causa tolli
volebat neque salutem suam Gallorum equitatui com-
mittere audebat, commodissimum esse statuit, omnibus
equis Gallis equitibus detractis, eo legionarios milites
legionis decimae, cui quam maxime confidebat, im-
20 ponere, ut praesidium quam amicissimum, si quid opus
facto esset, haberet. Quod cum fieret, non irridicule
quidam ex militibus decimae legionis dixit : plus quam
pollicitus esset Caesarem ei facere; pollicitum se in
cohortis praetoriae loco decimam legionem habiturum,
25 ad equum rescribere.

XLIII

Planities erat magna et in ea tumulus terrenus satis
grandis. Hic locus aequo fere spatio ab castris Ariovisti
et Caesaris aberat. Eo, ut erat dictum, ad colloquium
venerunt. Legionem Caesar quam equis vexerat passibus
ducentis ab eo tumulo constituit. Item equites Ariovisti 5
pari intervallo constiterunt. Ariovistus ex equis ut collo-
querentur et praeter se denos ut ad colloquium adduce-
rent postulavit. Ubi eo ventum est, Caesar initio orationis
sua senatusque in eum beneficia commemoravit, quod
rex appellatus esset a senatu, quod amicus, quod munera 10
amplissime missa; quam rem et paucis contigisse, et pro
magnis hominum officiis consuesse tribui docebat.
Illum, cum neque aditum neque causam postulandi
iustam haberet, beneficio ac liberalitate sua ac senatus ea
praemia consecutum. Docebat etiam quam veteres 15
quamque iustae causae necessitudinis ipsis cum Aeduis
intercederent; quae senatus consulta, quotiens quamque
honorifica in eos facta essent; ut omni tempore totius
Galliae principatum Aedui tenuissent, prius etiam quam
nostram amicitiam appetissent. Populi Romani hanc 20
esse consuetudinem, ut socios atque amicos non modo
sui nihil deperdere sed gratia, dignitate, honore auctiores
velit esse : quod vero ad amicitiam populi Romani
attulissent, id eis eripi quis pati posset ? Postulavit
deinde eadem quae legatis in mandatis dederat : ne aut 25
Aeduis aut eorum sociis bellum inferret; obsides redderet;
si nullam partem Germanorum domum remittere
posset, at ne quos amplius Rhenum transire pateretur.

XLIV

Ariovistus ad postulata Caesaris pauca respondit, de
suis virtutibus multa praedicavit : transisse Rhenum sese

non sua sponte sed rogatum et accersitum a Gallis; non
sine magna spe magnisque praemiis domum propinquos-
5 que reliquisse; sedes habere in Gallia ab ipsis concessas,
obsides ipsorum voluntate datos; stipendium capere iure
belli quod victores victis imponere consuerint. Non sese
Gallis sed Gallos sibi bellum intulisse; omnis Galliae
civitates ad se oppugnandum venisse ac contra se castra
10 habuisse; eas omnis copias a se uno proelio pulsas ac
superatas esse. Si iterum experiri velint, se iterum para-
tum esse decertare; si pace uti velint, iniquum esse de
stipendio recusare quod sua voluntate ad id tempus
pependerint. Amicitiam populi Romani sibi ornamento
15 et praesidio, non detrimento, esse oportere, idque se ea
spe petisse. Si per populum Romanum stipendium
remittatur et dediticii subtrahantur, non minus libenter
sese recusaturum populi Romani amicitiam, quam
appetierit. Quod multitudinem Germanorum in Galliam
20 traducat, id se sui muniendi, non Galliae impugnandae
causa facere : eius rei testimonium esse quod nisi rogatus
non venerit, et quod bellum non intulerit sed defenderit.
Se prius in Galliam venisse quam populum Romanum.
Numquam ante hoc tempus exercitum populi Romani
25 Galliae provinciae finibus egressum. Quid sibi vellet,
cur in suas possessiones veniret ? Provinciam suam
hanc esse Galliam, sicut illam nostram. Ut ipsi concedi
non oporteret, si in nostros finis impetum faceret, sic
item nos esse iniquos quod in suo iure se interpellaremus.
30 Quod fratres Aeduos appellatos diceret, non se tam
barbarum neque tam imperitum esse rerum ut non
sciret neque bello Allobrogum proximo Aeduos Romanis
auxilium tulisse neque ipsos in eis contentionibus quas
Aedui secum et cum Sequanis habuissent auxilio populi
35 Romani usos esse. Debere se suspicari simulata Cae-

sarem amicitia, quod exercitum in Gallia habeat, sui opprimendi causa habere. Qui nisi decedat atque exercitum deducat ex his regionibus, sese illum non pro amico sed hoste habiturum. Quod si eum interfecerit, multis sese nobilibus principibusque populi Romani gratum esse 40 facturum : id se ab ipsis per eorum nuntios compertum habere, quorum omnium gratiam atque amicitiam eius morte redimere posset. Quod si discessisset et liberam possessionem Galliae sibi tradidisset, magno se illum praemio remuneraturum et quaecumque bella geri vellet 45 sine ullo eius labore et periculo confecturum.

XLV

Multa ab Caesare in eam sententiam dicta sunt quare negotio desistere non posset : neque suam neque populi Romani consuetudinem pati uti optime merentis socios desereret, neque se iudicare Galliam potius esse Ariovisti quam populi Romani. Bello superatos esse Arvernos et 5 Rutenos ab Q. Fabio Maximo, quibus populus Romanus ignovisset neque in provinciam redegisset neque stipendium imposuisset. Quod si antiquissimum quodque tempus spectari oporteret, populi Romani iustissimum esse in Gallia imperium : si iudicium senatus observari 10 oporteret, liberam debere esse Galliam, quam bello victam suis legibus uti voluisset.

XLVI

Dum haec in colloquio geruntur, Caesari nuntiatum est equites Ariovisti propius tumulum accedere et ad nostros adequitare, lapides telaque in nostros coicere. Caesar loquendi finem facit seque ad suos recepit suisque imperavit ne quod omnino telum in hostis reicerent. Nam 5

etsi sine ullo periculo legionis delectae cum equitatu
proelium fore videbat, tamen committendum non putabat
ut, pulsis hostibus, dici posset eos ab se per fidem in
colloquio circumventos. Posteaquam in vulgus militum
10 elatum est qua arrogantia in colloquio Ariovistus usus
omni Gallia Romanis interdixisset, impetumque in
nostros eius equites fecissent, eaque res colloquium ut
diremisset, multo maior alacritas studiumque pugnandi
maius exercitui iniectum est.

CH. 47. *Ariovistus asks for another parley, either with
Caesar or his representative. Caesar sends a loyal Gaul,
C. Valerius Procillus, and a friend of Ariovistus, M.
Mettius. Ariovistus loses his temper and arrests them.*

XLVII

Biduo post Ariovistus ad Caesarem legatos mittit : velle
se de eis rebus quae inter eos agi coeptae neque perfectae
essent agere cum eo : uti aut iterum colloquio diem con-
stitueret aut, si id minus vellet, e suis legatis aliquem ad
5 se mitteret. Colloquendi Caesari causa visa non est, et eo
magis quod pridie eius diei Germani retineri non poterant
quin in nostros tela coicerent. Legatum e suis sese magno
cum periculo ad eum missurum et hominibus feris obiec-
turum existimabat. Commodissimum visum est C. Vale-
10 rium Procillum, C. Valeri Caburi filium, summa virtute
et humanitate adulescentem, cuius pater a C. Valerio
Flacco civitate donatus erat, et propter fidem et propter
linguae Gallicae scientiam, qua multa iam Ariovistus
longinqua consuetudine utebatur, et quod in eo peccandi
15 Germanis causa non esset, ad eum mittere, et M.
Mettium, qui hospitio Ariovisti utebatur. His mandavit

ut quae diceret Ariovistus cognoscerent et ad se referrent. Quos cum apud se in castris Ariovistus conspexisset, exercitu suo praesente conclamavit: Quid ad se venirent? An speculandi causa? Conantis dicere prohibuit et in 20 catenas coiecit.

CHS. 48–50. *Ariovistus moves his forces to try to cut Caesar's line of communication. Caesar repeatedly offers battle, but Ariovistus only engages in cavalry skirmishes. The German method of fighting with mixed forces of infantry and cavalry. Caesar constructs a second camp to restore his lines, and beats off Ariovistus's attempt to stop him. An engagement with part of Ariovistus's force: the Germans' reason for refusing a decisive battle.*

XLVIII

Eodem die castra promovit et milibus passuum sex a Caesaris castris sub monte consedit. Postridie eius diei praeter castra Caesaris suas copias traduxit et milibus passuum duobus ultra eum castra fecit, eo consilio uti frumento commeatuque qui ex Sequanis et Aeduis 5 supportaretur Caesarem intercluderet. Ex eo die dies continuos quinque Caesar pro castris suas copias produxit et aciem instructam habuit, ut, si vellet Ariovistus proelio contendere, ei potestas non deesset. Ariovistus his omnibus diebus exercitum castris continuit, equestri 10 proelio cotidie contendit. Genus hoc erat pugnae, quo se Germani exercuerant. Equitum milia erant sex, totidem numero pedites velocissimi ac fortissimi, quos ex omni copia singuli singulos suae salutis causa delegerant; cum his in proeliis versabantur. Ad eos se 15 equites recipiebant : hi, si quid erat durius, concurrebant;

si qui graviore vulnere accepto equo deciderat, circum-
sistebant; si quo erat longius prodeundum aut celerius
recipiendum, tanta erat horum exercitatione celeritas ut
20 iubis equorum sublevati cursum adaequarent.

XLIX

Ubi eum castris se tenere Caesar intellexit, ne diutius
commeatu prohiberetur, ultra eum locum, quo in loco
Germani consederant, circiter passus sescentos ab his,
castris idoneum locum delegit acieque triplici instructa
5 ad eum locum venit. Primam et secundam aciem in
armis esse, tertiam castra munire iussit. Hic locus ab
hoste circiter passus sescentos, uti dictum est, aberat.
Eo circiter hominum numero sedecim milia expedita
cum omni equitatu Ariovistus misit, quae copiae nostros
10 perterrerent et munitione prohiberent. Nihilo setius
Caesar, ut ante constituerat, duas acies hostem pro-
pulsare, tertiam opus perficere iussit. Munitis castris,
duas ibi legiones reliquit et partem auxiliorum; quattuor
reliquas in castra maiora reduxit.

L

Proximo die instituto suo Caesar e castris utrisque
copias suas eduxit paulumque a maioribus castris
progressus aciem instruxit; hostibus pugnandi potestatem fecit. Ubi ne tum quidem eos prodire intellexit,
5 circiter meridiem exercitum in castra reduxit. Tum
demum Ariovistus partem suarum copiarum quae castra
minora oppugnaret misit. Acriter utrimque usque ad
vesperum pugnatum est. Solis occasu suas copias
Ariovistus, multis et inlatis et acceptis vulneribus, in
10 castra reduxit. Cum ex captivis quaereret Caesar quam

ob rem Ariovistus proelio non decertaret, hanc reperiebat causam, quod apud Germanos ea consuetudo
esset ut matres familiae eorum sortibus et vaticinationi-
bus declararent utrum proelium committi ex usu esset
necne; eas ita dicere : non esse fas Germanos superare, si 15
ante novam lunam proelio contendissent.

Chs. 51-53. *Caesar forces the Germans to fight.
Description of the German host. A bitter and desperate
struggle; P. Crassus acts promptly and sends in the reserves
at the right moment. The Germans break and flee. Escape
of Ariovistus; rescue of Procillus and Mettius.*

LI

Postridie eius diei Caesar praesidium utrisque castris
quod satis esse visum est reliquit; omnis alarios in
conspectu hostium pro castris minoribus constituit, quod
minus multitudine militum legionariorum pro hostium
numero valebat, ut ad speciem alariis uteretur; ipse 5
triplici instructa acie usque ad castra hostium accessit.
Tum demum necessario Germani suas copias castris
eduxerunt generatimque constituerunt paribus intervallis,
Harudes, Marcomanos, Triboces, Vangiones, Nemetes,
Sedusios, Suebos, omnemque aciem suam raedis et 10
carris circumdederunt, ne qua spes in fuga relinquererut.
Eo mulieres imposuerunt, quae in proelium proficiscentis
passis manibus flentes implorabant ne se in servitutem
Romanis traderent.

LII

Caesar singulis legionibus singulos legatos et quaestorem praefecit, uti eos testis suae quisque virtutis haberet;

ipse a dextro cornu, quod eam partem minime firmam
hostium esse animadverterat, proelium commisit. Ita
5 nostri acriter in hostis signo dato impetum fecerunt,
itaque hostes repente celeriterque procurrerunt, ut
spatium pila in hostis coiciendi non daretur. Reiectis
pilis comminus gladiis pugnatum est. At Germani
celeriter ex consuetudine sua phalange facta impetus
10 gladiorum exceperunt. Reperti sunt complures nostri
milites qui in phalangas insilirent et scuta manibus
revellerent et desuper vulnerarent. Cum hostium acies a
sinistro cornu pulsa atque in fugam conversa esset, a
dextro cornu vehementer multitudine suorum nostram
15 aciem premebant. Id cum animadvertisset P. Crassus
adulescens, qui equitatui praeerat, quod expeditior erat
quam ei qui inter aciem versabantur, tertiam aciem
laborantibus nostris subsidio misit.

LIII

Ita proelium restitutum est, atque omnes hostes terga
verterunt neque prius fugere destiterunt quam ad flumen
Rhenum milia passuum ex eo loco circiter quindecim*
pervenerunt. Ibi perpauci aut viribus confisi tranare con-
5 tenderunt aut lintribus inventis sibi salutem reppererunt.
In his fuit Ariovistus, qui naviculam deligatam ad ripam
nactus ea profugit : reliquos omnis equitatu consecuti
nostri interfecerunt. Duae fuerunt Ariovisti uxores, una
Sueba natione, quam domo secum duxerat, altera Norica,
10 regis Voccionis soror, quam in Gallia duxerat a fratre
missam : utraeque in ea fuga perierunt ; duae filiae :
harum altera occisa, altera capta est. C. Valerius Procillus, cum a custodibus in fuga trinis catenis vinctus
traheretur, in ipsum Caesarem hostis equitatu per-

* *Oxford text* quinque

sequentem incidit. Quae quidem res Caesari non 15
minorem quam ipsa victoria voluptatem attulit, quod
hominem honestissimum provinciae Galliae, suum
familiarem et hospitem, ereptum e manibus hostium sibi
restitutum viderat, neque eius calamitate de tanta
voluptate et gratulatione quicquam fortuna deminuerat. 20
Is se praesente de se ter sortibus consultum dicebat
utrum igni statim necaretur an in aliud tempus reser-
varetur : sortium beneficio se esse incolumem. Item
M. Mettius repertus et ad eum reductus est.

Сн. 54. *Break-up and departure of Germans waiting
to join Ariovistus; the Ubii, a rival German tribe, severely
maul them on their retreat. Caesar leaves his troops, under
Labienus, in winter-quarters in Sequanian territory, and
himself returns to Cisalpine Gaul to pass the winter and
attend to civil affairs.*

LIV

Hoc proelio trans Rhenum nuntiato, Suebi qui ad
ripas Rheni venerant domum reverti coeperunt; quos
Ubii qui proximi Rhenum incolunt perterritos* insecuti
magnum ex eis numerum occiderunt. Caesar, una aestate
duobus maximis bellis confectis, maturius paulo quam 5
tempus anni postulabat in hiberna in Sequanos exercitum deduxit, hibernis Labienum praeposuit; ipse in
citeriorem Galliam ad conventus agendos profectus est.

* *This word is followed in the Oxford text by* [senserunt]

NOTES

I

This chapter gives a short geographical and ethnographical sketch of Gaul. It is meant to focus the minds of readers on the essential facts of the Gallic and German situation.

1. **Gallia.** In Caesar's time, this might mean either Cisalpine Gaul—Northern Italy—or the Roman 'province' of Gallia Transalpina, also called Narbonensis, Ulterior, and Bracata ('where-they-wear-breeches'); or, more generally, *the whole area* where the Gauls lived—modern France, with part of the Low Countries, Switzerland, and Northern Italy besides. Caesar here means *the whole area.*

1. **omnis.** Not ' all Gaul ' but ' viewed as a whole.'

3, 4. **lingua, institutis, legibus.** The Aquitanians were of mixed Gallic-Iberian blood; the central Gauls were almost purely Celtic; the Belgae were affected by the Germans. Thus ' language, customs, and laws ' would naturally differ.

7. **cultu atque humanitate provinciae . . .** ' the province, with its civilised way of life.'

8. **mercatores.** Romans, Greeks (from Massilia and elsewhere), and of other nations too. With the Romans, as with modern peoples, trade generally went ahead of colonial expansion. Ancient trade went far outside the Mediterranean basin.

8. **minimeque.** Translate with *saepe.*

9. **ad effeminandos animos.** A comfortable life make peoples turn from warfare and wish to settle down : ' wares which tend to weaken a people's warlike spirit.'

15–19. eorum . . . septentriones. *eorum* is vague; it means rather ' the country ' than ' the peoples.' Translate ' the part of Gaul . . . '

18. ab Sequanis et Helvetiis. ' *towards* the country of the Sequani and Helvetii ' (i.e. ' looked at *from* . . . ').

20. inferiorem partem. i.e. the part nearer its mouth.

23. ad Hispaniam. ' near Spain ' : the Bay of Biscay.

23, 24. inter occasum solis et septentriones. ' The north-west.' We should say that Aquitania faced the west, but, in Caesar's time, Spain was thought to project much more towards Ireland than it really does, thus pushing the Bay of Biscay round very much to the north-west.

II

2. M. Messalla, M. Pupio Pisone consulibus. i.e. 61 B.C.

3. inductus . . . fecit. Latin generally prefers a personal subject: we might say ' his ambition led him to form a plot . . . '

5. perfacile esse. Understand a verb of ' saying ' from ' persuasit.'

6, 7. hoc facilius . . . quod: (by so much) ' the more easily, because . . . '

7. loci natura. ' natural barriers.'

16. gloria belli atque fortitudinis. ' their proud reputation as brave soldiers.'

17. milia passuum. 13 *milia passuum*=(approx.) 12 English miles. The Helvetian territory extended roughly from the Pas de l'Ecluse to the junction of the Rhine and Aar (breadth), and from the same point to the southern end of Lake Constance (length). (The Aar is the river running N.E. along the south side of the Jura on map, pp. viii, ix.)

III

1. **rebus.** ' considerations.'

2. **pertinerent.** ' which, *they reckoned*, were needed for . . . ' : subjunctive because really in Indirect Statement —it is what they decided (*constituerunt*).

7, 8. **in tertium annum.** 'for two years later' : the Romans reckoned the year from which the counting begins. If Orgetorix's plot was made in 61 B.C., the decision of the Helvetians would be made later that year or in early 60. This gives 60 and 59 (two years' harvests) for preparation, and 58 for the departure. The final ' D-day ' was March 28th, 58 B.C. (ch. vi, lines 16, 17).

6, 8. **ad eas res conficiendas.** Repeated twice in three lines—an unrevised or unnoticed roughness.

10. **suscepit.** The tenses of this chapter vary between the ' natural ' past tenses (*constituerunt, duxerunt, suscepit,* etc.), and ' vivid ' present tenses (*confirmant, deligitur, etc.*).

10, 11. **Casticus, Catamantaloedes.** Evidently Catamantaloedes was dethroned by the council of the Sequani, or perhaps no ' king ' was appointed in his place after his death.

12, 13. **populi Romani amicus.** A complimentary title, often given by the Senate to foreign rulers.

10, 14. **persuadet . . . ut occuparet.** *persuadet* is 'vivid' present referring to past time: hence the sequence of tenses; cf *persuadet ut conaretur* ' below.

15. **eo tempore.** It is now 60 B.C.

15. **principatum.** ' chief magistracy.'

20. **non esse dubium.** Verb of ' saying ' understood from *probat*.

20. **totius Galliae.** In ch. 1 (see note) *eorum* stood for the *country* : here, the name of the country stands for its *peoples*.

21. **illis.** Casticus and Dumnorix.

23. **regno occupato,** ' if they seized . . . ' : with all down to ' populos.'

24, 25. **sese . . . posse sperant.** *Possum* has no future infir.itive—' hoped that they could ' (as in English).

IV

1. **per indicium,** ' by (the action of) an informer.'

2. **ex vinclis.** We should say ' *in* chains.'

5. **familiam.** *Not* ' family ' but ' clan,' ' followers.'

6. **obaeratos.** ' Bondmen '—men forced by poverty or debt to ' bind ' themselves to the service of a powerful noble.

8. **civitas.** This means ' the people '; but the lead in bringing Orgetorix to justice would be taken by the tribal council, of nobles, warriors, and druids. They ' brought in a multitude ' of the common people to enforce their decision.

V

For the geography of chs. v–xxix, which describe Caesar's operations against the Helvetians, see the map on page 42.

1, 2. **id quod constituerant . . . conantur . . . ut exeant.** Caesar mixes ' vivid ' present tenses (*conantur, exeant*) with a ' natural ' pluperfect (*constituerant*) in one dependent clause.

3. **oppida.** Walled towns, often built on hills for easier defence.

4. **vicos.** Unfortified hamlets and villages.

6. **comburunt.** The main verb is again a ' vivid ' present : the dependent verb, *essent*, is in the ' natural ' historic tense.

8. mensum. Third decl. nouns in *-is* (e.g. *civis*) generally have their gen. pl. in *-ium*: but *mensum*, not *mensium*, was generally written in Caesar's time.

11, 12. oppidis ... exustis ... proficiscantur. Say ' to burn ... and march.' Study in this sentence the combination of ' vivid ' and ' historic ' tenses.

12. Boios. Worthy of special note.

VI

2, 3. unum ... Rhodanum : i.e. the Pas de l'Ecluse:

3, 4. vix qua ... ducerentur. Take *qua* first: *ducerentur* is ' result ' subjunctive.

8. qui nuper pacati erant. The Allobroges rose against Rome in 61 B.C., and were taught a sharp lesson, which they still resented.

13. viderentur. Subjunctive in reported speech, dependent on *existimabant*.

15. diem dicunt, qua die. Caesar often repeats ' day ' after a relative pronoun.

16. conveniant. Purpose subjunctive : ' ... for all to muster ... '.

16, 17. a. d. V Kal. Apr. L. Pisone, A. Gabinio consulibus. March 28th, 58 B.C.

VII

1, 2. Caesari cum id ... conari. The accusative and infinitive explains ' *id*,' and depends on *nuntiatum esset*. ' When news reached Caesar that ... '

2. ab urbe. Rome; he had not yet left to take up his governorship.

3. quam maximis potest itineribus. Here *iter* means ' stage ' : Caesar was not travelling with his whole force, only with his staff from Rome.   One legion was already ' in the Province ' and three at Aquileia (ch. x).

3. **Galliam ulteriorem.**   Right through Northern Italy (*Gallia Cisalpina* or *Citerior*) to ' further ' or Transalpine Gaul.   For the moment, he is concerned with the ' Province ' :   he will soon have to think of Gaul outside the Province.

4. **ad Genavam.**   *Not*   ' reached   Geneva '—this would take no preposition;   ' . . . *the vicinity of* Geneva.'

5. **imperat.**   ' levied.'

6. **legio una.**   At full strength, the legion might have 6,000 men (roughly equivalent to a British brigade), with attendant (allied) auxiliaries and cavalry.   On active service, the legions were often much below full strength.

6, 7. **pontem . . . rescindi.**   See ch. vi : the first step for defence.

12. **haberent.**   Subjunctive in dependent clause in Indirect Statement.

12. **rogare.**   Perhaps understand *se* (from *sibi*)—' they said that they asked ' :   *or* (more likely) historic infinitive —' they asked.'

14. **L. Cassium.**   The Helvetians brought to Caesar's mind the great deeds of the Tigurini against Cassius, less than sixty years before;   old Divico (ch. xiii), then the leader of the Tigurini, was still with them;   and this gives Caesar a chance of referring to the previous defeat, both by way of propaganda (he did better than Cassius) and to show how he wiped out an old score.

15. **sub iugum missum.**   Two javelins were fixed in the ground, with a third fastened across, to make a small arch.   The beaten army had to march through, under the mockery and blows of the victors.

15, 16. **concedendum.**   Understand *sibi esse.*

17. **data facultate.**   ' If given the opportunity . . . '

19, 20. **dum . . . convenirent.** Purpose subjunctive.

20. **diem.** Not ' take a day to consider ' (this would
need *unum diem*), but ' choose a date for discussion.'
Caesar openly says that he was playing for time (*dum
milites convenirent*).

21. **reverterentur.** ' Command ' subjunctive in past
time : ' they should . . . '

VIII

5. **murum.** Along the Rhône. The ' wall ' was not
continuous, nor did it need to be. Caesar needed only to
fortify the weak spots—the ' many fords ' mentioned in
ch. vi.

4, 5. **decem novem.** Rare for *undeviginti*. This was
the usual Roman method of making defence-works. A
ditch or trench (*fossa*) was dug and the earth piled in a
ridge (*agger* or *vallum*) often strengthened with stakes
(*valli*).

6. **praesidia . . . castella.** Small bodies of troops—
' pickets '—to watch, and give the alarm. They ' sat in
front of ' (*prae* + *sedeo*) the fortification. The *castella* were
fortified strongpoints, bases for resistance or rallying points
when the troops were pressed. The Romans did not man
a defence line continuously, but from forts spaced along it.

8, 9. **ubi ea dies . . . venit.** Were the Helvetians taken
in by Caesar's offer of negotiation ? It is now more than a
fortnight (April 13th) after their original D-day (March
28th).

9, 10. **negat se more et exemplo p. R. . . .** Caesar
is ready and confident : ' it would, he said, be against
all the traditions and customs of Rome for him to . . . '

12. **ea spe.** Of being granted a right of way.

12. **navibus iunctis.** ' By bridges of boats.' Understand, with these words, *alii* to balance *alii vadis*. These

were not full-scale attacks, but isolated thrusts of small determined bands.

14, 15. si . . . possent. 'In the hope that they might . . .'

15, 16. militum concursu. The Roman troops did their job. See the note on *praesidia* above.

IX

1. relinquebatur. Where the verb comes early in the sentence, it is often good to say ' there was . . . '

1. una . . . via. The Pas de l'Ecluse

3. Dumnorigem. Again involved in doubtful transactions. As he had plotted with Orgetorix, we might have expected the Helvetians to think twice before asking him for help.

4. eo deprecatore. Either ' ablative absolute '— with him as their pleader—or, rather, ablative (instrumental) of means—' through his good offices.'

6. plurimum poterat. ' . . . had much influence among the Sequani, where he had spent money lavishly to gain favour.' Dumnorix was a prominent Aeduan, but wished to be more, and was jealous of his elder brother, Diviciacus (ch. xx). The Sequani had been hostile to the Aedui. Dumnorix looks for help outside his own people.

11. obsides. The normal way for two tribes to confirm an agreement was to exchange hostages as security.

X

2. Santonum fines. On the Bay of Biscay, north of the Garonne estuary. The Helvetians are still thinking of the exploits of the Tigurini, 50 years before.

4-7. magno cum periculo provinciae futurum ut . . . haberet. ' It must cause great danger to the Province, that (if) it should have . . . '

6. **patentibus.** Exposed, easily attacked; Caesar was right in foreseeing the danger.

8. **T. Labienum.** The first mention of Caesar's great second-in-command. **legatum.** 'Deputy' or 'representative,' one to whom responsibility is 'delegated.' Caesar's 'legates' were expected to do any task their commander might prescribe, and did not necessarily hold a permanent position.

8. **in Italiam.** i.e. Cisalpine Gaul; Caesar had no authority outside his provinces.

9. **duas legiones.** The Eleventh and Twelfth. Caesar raised these troops without orders from Rome, and did not get a grant for their pay till two years later.

11. **qua proximum iter.** See map p. 42. The shortest way is now by Briançon (Brigantio) and Grenoble, but the Vocontii lie further to the south. Caesar probably went from Briançon by way of Embrun, Gap, Chorges, and Die, perhaps because of the resistance of the mountain people (always troublesome), perhaps because there was no satisfactory road by Grenoble.

12, 13. **ire contendit.** ('made great efforts to go') 'hurried.'

16. **citerioris provinciae.** Cisalpine Gaul. The position of *Ocelum* has been disputed, but is almost certainly at the modern Drubiaglio.

17. **die septimo.** He kept up a rate of more than twenty miles a day in difficult country, against opposition, with nearly half his force consisting of newly-enlisted troops.

18. **in Segusiavos.** The danger affects more than the 'Province,' and Caesar strikes beyond the frontiers.

XI

1–3. **Helvetii . . . populabantur.** The description of the *Arar* (Saône) (ch. xii) probably gives their route.

3–4. **cum non possent.** When *cum* takes the subjunctive there is some other idea implied than simply ' when.' Here it is reason : ' failing to . . .' or ' being unable to . . .'

5. **rogatum.** Accusative of supine after verb of motion (*mittunt*), expressing purpose.

6. **meritos esse.** Understand a verb of 'saying' from *rogatum*: ' saying that . . .'

5, 6. **ita . . . ut.** ' So *well* . . . that . . .'

8, 9. **Aedui Ambarri.** Why does Caesar say ' the Aeduan Ambarri ' and then repeat that they were ' related to the Aedui ' ? Perhaps the word *quo* should come after *tempore*, then it would mean ' at the same time *as* the Aedui (appealed), the Ambarri also . . .' Perhaps ' Aedui ' should be omitted.

11. **Allobroges.** A small area north of the Rhône, near Ambérieu, was held by the Allobroges.

15–17. **dum . . . pervenirent.** ' Until they *should* . . .' *dum*, with the subjunctive, almost implies result.

16. **Santonos.** Caesar uses the gen. pl. *Santonum* (from *Santones*, 3rd decl.) in ch. x.

XII

2. **incredibili lenitate.** See the first note on ch. xi This description fits the Saône between Trévoux and Thoissey. The contrast between the sluggish Saône and the swift Rhône, at their junction at Lyon, is most striking.

4. **transibant.** i.e. by bridges of boats (*iunctis*).

7. **de tertia vigilia.** The Romans divided the day into twelve hours, from sunrise to sunset; the night into four ' watches ' (*vigiliae*) of about three hours each. This probably means ' about *the start of* the third watch '— i.e. soon after midnight.

8. **profectus.** Caesar's camp was probably on the heights above Sathonay, just north of the confluence of Rhône and Saône at *Lugdunum* (Lyon). He had only a few miles to go, through country which would screen his approach; but how much more skilful was his operation than that of the Helvetians (*inopinantis*).

12. **Tigurinus pagus.** See ch. vii. *pagus*, a sub-division of the Helvetian people : ' canton.'

16–19. **sive casu . . . persolvit.** Caesar's reference to history is artistically complete, and Heaven is invoked as Rome's ally.

19. **princeps.** ' was the first to . . . '

XIII

2. **pontem.** i.e. of boats. He was not opposed; the Helvetians were proceeding in a haphazard fashion, and he had destroyed their rearguard.

5. **ut . . . transirent.** Explains *id quod*, ' in crossing ' —' to cross.'

6. **legatos.** Choose a more suitable word than ' ambassadors.'

7. **Divico.** If Divico fought in the *bellum Cassianum*, forty-nine years before (Introduction, p. 14), he must by now have been a very old man.

8. **egit.** ' argued.'

8–11. **si . . . voluisset.** Indirect statement after *egit*. This goes on to the end of the chapter.

9. **in eam partem ituros, etc.** Understand *esse*. This is a remarkable ' offer'; did the Helvetians really mean it, or were they playing for time ?

12, 16. **reminisceretur, tribueret, despiceret.** Commands in Indirect Statement ; ' let him . . .' or ' he should . . . '

13. quod. (' as to the fact that . . . ') ' Perhaps he had . . . , *but* . . . '

18. insidiis. A sneer at Caesar's scientific warfare.

19. committeret. Again, command; ' . . . act.'

20, 21. nomen . . . proderet. The Romans did not forget their defeats.

XIV

1, 2. eo . . . minus . . . quod. 'All the less . . . because . . . '; correlatives.

3. eo gravius . . . quo minus. Again, correlatives; take *quo minus* first; ' because Rome had so little deserved . . . he was all the more . . . '

4. qui. The Roman people : ' if they . . . '

5. fuisse. Indirect statement, as is nearly all this chapter : stands for *fuisset* in direct statement.

5, 6. deceptum. Again, the Roman people. Understand *esse*. ' but they had been deceived . . . ' *eo . . . quod, etc.* ' by the fact that they knew of nothing they had done which might give them reason for fear . . . . '

7. timendum. Understand *esse*.

7. quod si. Not ' but if ': either omit *quod*, or say as to that, if . . . '

8. vellet. The subject is now Caesar himself.

8–11. num . . . posse. The usual way of putting a ' rhetorical ' question (one not expecting an answer) in indirect statement is by the accusative and infinitive. *posse* has no subject, and *se* must be supplied : ' *could* he . . . ' (Caesar).

10, 11. Allobrogas. This is really a Greek name (the Greeks were in Gaul long before the Romans—remember Massilia), and this is the Greek 3rd decl. acc. pl.

11, 12. **quod, quodque.** ' The fact that they . . . and . . . '

14. **consuesse.** i.e. *consuevisse.*

14, 15. **quo . . . doleant.** Purpose containing a comparative—' by which they might . . . the more '; say ' so that they might . . . more . . . ' *Doleant* is ' vivid ' present; this is a ' general ' statement, always true (also *velint*).

15, 16. **quos . . . eis.** Latin often puts the relative *before* the ' antecedent.' Take *eis . . . concedere* first.

23. **consuerint.** ' Vivid ' perfect, with present meaning; ' *were* accustomed.'

XV

2. **equitatum:** allied troops. See the Introduction, p. 17.

4. **qui videant:** purpose.

5. **qui cupidius . . . cadunt.** Dumnorix was in command of the Aeduan cavalry; *was* he reliable ? See ch. xviii.

10. **non numquam.** ' Repeatedly.'

12, 13. **rapinis pabulationibus populationibusque.** Irregular latinity. When three or more words are thus joined, ' and ' is generally placed between each, or entirely omitted.

14. **iter fecerunt.** The Helvetii first marched along the west bank of the Saône. The direct way to the land of the Santoni was too difficult for their wagons.

15, 16. **quinis aut senis m. p.** Five or six miles *on any day*—distributive numerals.

XVI

1. **essent.** Subj. in indirect statement, dependent on *flagitare.*

2. **flagitare.** ' Historic ' infinitive, often used ' vividly ' for the indicative. So also *ducere, dicere*, below.

4. **frumenta.** The plural always means ' standing corn,' ' crops (in the fields).'

6. **navibus.** In Caesar's day there was regular traffic of large barges. See note on ch. xviii.

7, 8. **iter . . . averterant.** Near Mâcon.

8. **diem ex die.** *diem:* accusative of 'time how long'; the object of *ducere* is ' *Caesarem*,' understood.

9. **conferri**—by individual contributors: **comportari** —the whole consignment.

13. **praeerat.** The manuscripts say **praeerant**, but there was only one ' vergobret ' at once.

16. **possit.** The manuscripts say **posset**; the tense is changed to fit with **accusat** and **sublevetur.**

XVII

2. **proponit: esse . . .** The whole chapter is in Indirect Speech after Liscus' opening, and ' vivid ' tenses are used.

2. **non nullos.** ' certain individuals '—(not a few).

4. **magistratus.** ' Officials ' rather than ' magistrates.'

9. **Aeduis.** Dative of ' disadvantage,' not ablative, but translate ' from the A.' The Romans always put the dative of the person ' deprived,' as he is really the indirect object.

9. **una cum,** ' together with . . . '

12. **quin.** Not the same as after *dubitare* (above): ' furthermore.'

12. **quod.** *Not* ' because,' but ' as to the fact that,' or ' in having told . . . '.

12. **necessariam rem.** This is a difficult sentence and the text is not above suspicion. If the reading

necessariam rem is correct, it must mean 'the unavoidable fact.' However, the phrase *necessaria re coactus* is found elsewhere and the ablative here has some authority. If we accept it, it would mean 'under compulsion,' merely expanding the meaning of *coactus*.

XVIII

4, 5. **quae ... dixerat.** *Not* 'asked him what he had said' (this would be subjunctive) but 'asked him (about) what he had said'—a relative clause.

6. **ipsum esse.** 'The person in question was none other than D.' All is now Indirect Statement, down to *desperare*.

7, 8. **audacia ... gratia.** Ablatives of 'description' —'with ...'; we say 'of ...', or 'who had ...'

9. **portoria ... vectigalia.** River-traffic, much used in Gaul, was subject to tolls. A regular way of collecting taxes in the ancient world was for a private individual to buy at auction the right of collecting the taxes.

10. **parvo pretio.** 'Gang' politics: Dumnorix threatened with violence any who might have bid against him.

14. **domi.** 'among his own people.'

15. **largiter.** A very rare word, used to echo *largiendum* 'By giving largesse got the largest power' (Professor J. C. Rolfe, quoted by Rice Holmes).

19. **nuptum.** Accusative of supine, for purpose : *collocasse* is virtually a verb of 'motion.'

21. **suo nomine.** 'on his own account.'

25. **venire.** Stands for '*veniat*' in Direct Statement— 'if anything *were to happen* ... he *would come* into good prospects (*spem*).' '*Si quid accidat*' is a polite understatement for 'if the Romans were beaten.'

25. **imperio p. R.** 'Under Roman authority ...'

27. quod. Again, *not* 'because,' but 'as regards the fact that . . .' Translate ' in the defeat of the cavalry . . .'

29. a Dumnorige atque . . . . Make the sentence active : ' it was D. and his cavalry who had begun . . . .'

XIX

2. certissimae res. 'indisputable facts.'

2. quod. 'that': how often *quod* means something other than 'because.'

3. traduxisset. This, and the other subordinate verbs in this sentence, are really in Indirect Statement (the idea comes from *suspiciones*), therefore subjunctive.

4. iniussu suo. 'without his orders' *et civitatis* 'and (those of) the state . . .'

8. his omnibus rebus. 'There was only one objection to all these suggestions.'

11, 12. ne Diviciaci animum offenderet. *Animum* need not be translated.

13. conaretur. 'Before he took any action.' Conjunctions of *time* (e.g. *priusquam*) take the indicative if they indicate *only* time; if any other idea is present, the subjunctive. Here there is an idea of motive ' to avoid the necessity for action.'

15. C. Valerium Procillum. 'A leading Gaul . . .,' who had been admitted to Roman citizenship.

17. simul. With *et ostendit* : ' he (at the same time) both . . . and . . .'

20. eius. Not with *animi*, but neuter, 'at it,' though it need not be translated: say ' without taking offence . . .'

21. causa cognita . . . statuat. 'To try the case *and* decide it.'

XX

Much of this chapter is in Indirect Statement. Down to *averterentur*, Diviciacus is speaking, and ' natural ' past tenses are used. Then, down to *dicit*, Caesar himself speaks, uses ' vivid ' tenses, and (again for vividness) uses many different verbs of ' saying.'

2. **gravius.** ' too . . . '

4. **propterea quod**—with *crevisset*; **cum**—with *posset,* whose subjects are both *ipse* (Diviciacus) and *ille* (Dumnorix). The conjunction is omitted for effect between the two subjects, and might be ' but.'—Remember the friction between Diviciacus and Dumnorix.

9. **existimatione vulgi.** ' Public opinion.' Dumnorix was very popular : see ch. xviii.

9. **quod si.** Here ' *but* if.'

10, 11. **ipse, sua.** Diviciacus.

12. **qua ex re futurum uti.** ' The result (of this) would be that . . . '

13. **pluribus verbis.** ' At considerable length ' : perhaps even ' more ' than Caesar quotes.

15. **rogat . . . faciat.** Indirect command : *ut* would be strictly correct, but it is often omitted.

21. **Diviciaco.** ' *for* his brother's sake ': indirect object of *condonare.*

22. **custodes.** *Not* ' guards,' but ' men to watch D.'

XXI

The operations against the Helvetians go on. See how systematically Caesar had followed the enemy right from the beginning, keeping his distance, and awaiting his chance.

3, 4. **qualis esset . . . qui cognoscerent . . . misit.**
Reverse the order : *misit* (*exploratores*) *qui cognoscerent*
(purpose) *qualis esset* (indirect question) . . .

3. **in circuitu.**   (probably) ' on different (various)
sides '; (possibly) ' on the other side.'

5. **de tertia vigilia.**   Another midnight march, as
against the Tigurini (ch. xii) : but this time Caesar plans
a ' pincers ' operation, sends Labienus 'first, and follows
himself about three hours later.

5. **legatum pro praetore.**   Second in rank only to
Caesar himself : Caesar was proconsul.

7, 8. **quid sui consili sit ostendit.** ' Explained what
his plan was.' *Consili* is ' partitive ' genitive, indistin-
guishable here from *quid suum consilium sit.*

8. **de quarta vigilia.**   He hopes to attack soon after
dawn : he has eight miles to go, and Labienus was to
seize the hill (the key to the situation).

10. **P. Considius.**   Splendid experience, but how poor
Considius hindered Caesar's plan!

XXII

1. **prima luce.**   The ' pincers ' are in position at the
right time.

1–4. **cum summus mons . . . cognitus esset.** As
so often with a long Latin sentence, a good way of trans-
lating is to omit *cum* altogether, make a number of short
principal clauses, with semicolons, and end with ' *but then*
Considius . . . '

6, 7. **a Gallicis armis atque insignibus.**   The *a* is
unusual.   We should normally expect either an instrumental ablative without a preposition or *ex* with the
ablative denoting the source of the information.

8. **in proximum collem.**   To wait for developments,
and for security.

11–12. **ut ... fieret.** Caesar's own words for his ' pincers ' plan.

13. **multo denique die.** ' It was broad day before ... ' *multo die* means ' when much of the day was past, '—*how* much, depends on the context. Considius's wrong report made Caesar think that his plan had miscarried ; so he secured his position (*in proximum collem copias subducit*), and sent scouts to reconnoitre. This would not take long, but too long for his original plan to be operated, for by this time (perhaps about 9 a.m.) the birds had flown; *cognovit Helvetios castra movisse.*

XXIII

1, 2. **supererat cum ... oporteret.** Still another meaning of *cum* : ' until the time when he would have to ... ', ' before ... '

2. **metiri.** again, probably used passively (see ch. xvi).

2, 3. **a Bibracte.** distance from, not motion from— hence the preposition.
Bibracte stood on the plateau of Mont Beauvray. Excavations made in the time of Napoleon III disclosed a city of about 333 acres in extent. This is larger than Roman London, which was by far the biggest city in Britain (325 acres). There were found fortifications; houses of stone, shops and tools of enamel-workers, native and imported pottery, and both Gallic and Roman coins. Most of the latter were dated before the Roman conquest; none of the Roman coins were later than 5 B.C.—probably the date when a move was made to a new site to the east called, after Augustus, Augustodunum (*Autun*).

5. **prospiciendum.** *esse* understood, as often with the ' gerund.'

7. **L. Aemili.** A Romanised Gaul or Roman officer placed in command of a *decuria* of cavalry (ten men).

9–12. **existimarent ... confiderent.** ' alleged' reason, so subjunctive.

12. **commutato consilio.** The Helvetians jump to the conclusion that Caesar is giving up.

XXIV

2. **qui   sustineret.** ' Purpose ' subjunctive.   The cavalry were to take the first shock of the Helvetian attack, and give Caesar time to arrange his troops *interim*.

3. **in colle medio.** ' half-way up . . . '

3, 4. **triplicem aciem.** The normal disposition.

5. **duas legiones . . . et auxilia.** The raw troops and the allies are to guard the baggage, and will only be used in an extremity.

7. **totum montem.** ' all the higher part of the hill ' —i.e. above the *acies*. This must mean that Caesar ordered the ' reserve ' and allied troops to ' deploy ' in open order, so as to occupy the whole of the ground described.

7. **sarcinas.** The soldiers' personal kit, tools, etc., not actually used in fighting.

9. **muniri.** As usual, by an earthwork (*fossa* + *vallum*). In 1886 was found a crescent-shaped trench, the distance between the ends being about 300 yards. It was shallow, seemed to have been hastily dug, and was unfinished ; it could well have been the earthwork here mentioned. Later discoveries of bones and weapons confirm the identification of the site of the battle.

11. **phalange facta.** The ' phalanx,' a Greek invention, consisted of a mass of heavy infantry advancing in close order to crush the enemy. In the Gallic phalanx the front rank held their shields overlapping in front, and the rows behind carried their shields over their heads, ready to lower them at need.

12. **sub.** ' up to . . . '

XXV

1. **omnium.** Not of the cavalry: only of the mounted officers, who were to fight on foot with the men.

4. **pilis missis.** Such a fire was deadly. The Roman defence was exactly according to the drill-book.

6–10. **Gallis . . . pugnare.** The *pilum* had a four-foot wooden shaft, with a heavy iron blade, also about four feet long, sometimes barbed, and with sharp cutting edges. This was fastened to the shaft by two rivets, one of wood. The latter easily broke when the point struck its target, so that the weapon bent without breaking, with the effect which Caesar here describes.

8. **cum . . . inflexisset.** ' *as* the point . . .'—reason, therefore subjunctive.

10. **multi ut.** Take *ut* first (=*ita ut*, result).

13. **mons.** ' another hill.'

13. **suberat.** ('was near ') 'was only . . . away.'

14. **capto monte.** Obviously ' reached,' *not* ' captured.'

16. **praesidio erant.** Dative of purpose.

16. **ex itinere.** The Celtic forces had been in a long straggling formation : the Boii and Tulingi, who ' were the rearguard,' attacked as soon as they arrived. But the fighting so far described could not have lasted long, and the Boii and Tulingi could not have had far to come : perhaps they were left on one side to guard the baggage, like Caesar's two new legions.

17. **latere aperto.** The ' open flank ' is the right, because the shield was carried on the left arm.

20. **conversa.** Really, only the *third* line ' wheeled ' or ' faced about ' : the first and second lines continued to engage the Helvetians (*ut victis et summotis resisteret*).

XXVI

3. **alteri**—the Helvetians, **alteri**—the Boii and Tulingi :
' the first part of the enemy . . . the other . . . '

5. **cum.** ' although.'

5. **ab hora septima.** About 1 p.m. The battle
probably lasted about seven hours, the second stage
(from the intervention of the Boii and Tulingi) being by
far the longer.

6. **aversum hostem.** ' turned in flight.'

6, 7. **ad multam noctem.** ' well into . . .', cf. *multo
die*, ch. xxii.

8. **pro vallo.** They formed a ' laager ' with their
wagons.

10. **mataras ac tragulas.** Pikes and javelins used by
the Gauls and Spaniards. The *tragula* was thrown by
means of a leather strap.

15, 16. **in finis Lingonum die quarto.** About eighty
miles in three days, remarkable for a beaten army. Non-
combatants must have suffered considerably.

19. **Lingonas.** Greek acc. pl.: see note on ch. xiv.

19, 20. **ne . . . iuvarent.** ' forbidding them to . . . '

20. **qui si . . . .** ' if they ' : and *iuvissent* (in indirect
statement) stands for *iuverint* (fut. perf.) in direct speech.

20, 21. **eodem loco . . . habiturum.** ' would regard
them *as enemies*, like . . . '

21. **triduo intermisso.** To bury the dead, reorganise
and re-equip his troops, etc.

XXVII

2. **in itinere.** We do not know just where. The
Helvetii probably turned east, towards their old home,
and this meeting may have been near Dijon.

10. **supplicio.** ' Punishment ' generally received in a ' suppliant ' position (as of prayer) : here, death.

13. **ignorari.** Not ' ignore.'

13. **existimarent.** ' Alleged ' reason, virtually indirect statement, as in ch. xxiii.

XXVIII

1. **quorum . . . his.** Take *his* (the ' antecedent ') first : ' . . . the peoples through whose . . . '

2. **sibi.** ' In his eyes ' : dative of ' person interested.'

3. **in hostium numero habuit.** ' treated them as . . . '; they were probably put to death : Caesar had to act effectively.

8. **frumenti copiam facerent.** The Helvetii had burnt all their surplus supplies (ch. v), and carried only ' iron rations,' probably long since eaten or lost. Caesar was merciful when he could be.

10. **ea maxime ratione.** ' His chief reason was . . . ' Sound policy : Ariovistus was already across the Rhine, and other Germans were massing (ch. xxxvii).

14. **Boios.** Object of *collocarent*: ' When the A. asked . . . because they . . . he . . . ' The Boii were a ' special case.'

14, 15. **petentibus Aeduis.** Abl. abs.

16. **illi.** The Aedui.

18. **atque.** ' as '—regularly so after *idem, aequus, par*, etc.

XXIX

1, 2. **litteris Graecis.** The Greek alphabet was often used by the Gauls.

5. **quarum omnium rerum.** ' Taken all together ' : summarises the entries in the Helvetian lists.

9, 10. **nonaginta duo . . . CCCLXVIII.** The number of combatants is exactly one-quarter of the total. Some scholars have accused Caesar of exaggeration; but there is no real reason to doubt his figures. Many would ' fall by the wayside ' : many wagons would be abandoned : the Tigurini (one-quarter of the Helvetii) were dealt with separately; and many would perish both in the battle at Toulon-sur-Arroux and in the flight. Further (see Introduction, p. 9), Caesar only says that these numbers were given in the Helvetian lists. Thus the figure of 130,000 survivors from the battle (ch. xxvi), and of 110,000 who returned home, may easily be correct.

XXX

The Helvetian danger is now removed, and the interest shifts to the other threat, from Ariovistus.

1. **totius fere Galliae.** Rather an exaggeration, but Caesar really means ' Celtic ' Gaul (see ch. 1).

2. **gratulatum.** Acc. of ' supine,' for purpose with verb of motion.

3. **intellegere sese.** The rest of the chapter is in indirect statement, the verb of ' saying ' being understood from *gratulatum*.

3, 4. **pro veteribus iniuriis.** In the *Bellum Cassianum*.

5, 6. **terrae Galliae.** *Galliae* in apposition to *terrae*. We had *lacu Lemanno* in ch. viii, l. 2.

7. **florentissimis rebus.** abl. abs.: ' at the height of their power.'

7. **eo consilio.** Taken up by *uti . . . haberent* : ' with the object of . . . '

10. **ex omni Gallia.** ' *In* . . . '

13. **diem.** Again, ' date.'

16. **concilio.** Dative of purpose : probably at Bibracte, the capital of the Aedui. Held there, it would

give Caesar great prestige amongst the Aedui, and give the Aedui (old allies of Rome) great prestige among the other Gauls.

XXXI

Nearly the whole chapter is in Indirect Statement.

3. **secreto.** The words *in occulto* are found in the manuscripts, but are omitted, as they mean little more than *secreto*. The chieftains were terrified, and desperately anxious that no-one should know, and said so.

5. **non minus . . . quam uti.** ' Just as . . . as . . . '

13. **mercede arcesserentur.** Thirteen years before, in 71 B.C.—or perhaps a little later (see note on ch. xxxvi).

16. **traductos.** Understand *esse*.

17. **ad.** Used as adverb (prepositions are very like adverbs) : ' about . . . '

20. **omnem.** An excited exaggeration; but points like this make Caesar's narrative so close to reality.

20. **nobilitatem.** ' chiefs '—the most prominent of the *equitatus*.

20. **equitatum.** Not 'cavalry' but knights (=men of rank).

21. **qui.** Concessive : ' although they . . . '

22. **hospitio.** A regular word for a treaty of friendship between Rome and another people.

29. **potuerit.** So far, all the dependent verbs have been in ' natural ' historic tenses. This is in the ' vivid ' perfect (primary) because Diviciacus is making a personal statement, almost in parenthesis—' I am the only . . . '; and the verbs dependent on it (*iuraret, daret*) are again historic.

35. **tertiam partem.** viz. Alsace.

39. **quibus . . . pararentur.** Perhaps purpose ' so that
. . . could be . . . for them ' : or (better?) command in past
time : ' for whom (let . . . be provided) they were ordered
to provide . . . '

40. **futurum esse.** ' The result would be that . . . '

44, 45. **ut sem 1 vicerit.** ' *when* once . . .': Caesar uses
vivid tenses for the rest of the reported speech, to emphasise
Diviciacus's vivid picture of the desperate situation.

45, 46. **Admagetobrigae.** Locative. The name is not
certain, and the manuscripts differ. ' *Ad Magetobrigam*
(near M.) ' has been suggested. This battle was fought
in 61 or 60 B.C.

47, 48. **omnia exempla cruciatusque.** ' Every kind
of punishment and torture.'

51. **nisi quid . . . auxili.** ' Partitive ' genitive—
' any(thing of) help,' ' some help.'

53. **ut emigrent.** Explains *id quod*: ' namely, to . . . '

XXXII

3. **unos** = *solos.*

6. **respondere.** Historic infinitive, used (often) vividly
for the indicative.

6, 7. **in eadem tristitia taciti.** ' . . . gloomy silence . . '

8. **idem.** ' The same man as before ': often it means
' again.'

9. **hoc.** Ablative of degree with the comparative :
' all the more . . . because . . . '

14. **tamen.** Concessive *adverb*, not conjunction : ' at
any rate . . . '

XXXIII

2. **sibi . . . curae futuram.** *curae* is ' predicative '
dative, ' that he would attend to it.'

3. **beneficio suo.** See ch. xxxv; Ariovistus had in Caesar's consulship, with Caesar's help, been honoured by the Senate with a complimentary title.

5. **secundum ea.** ' Besides (following) these considerations . . . '

6. **quare.** (' because of which he should ') ' to . . . '

8. **fratres . . . appellatos.** First in 123 B.C., for their services in Rome's conquest of the Province.

11. **in tanto imperio.** ' Considering the (so) great power . . . '

11. **quod.** ' A thing which . . . '

13. **consuescere.** This phrase is the subject of *periculosum* (*esse*), ' he saw that it was dangerous that the G. should . . . ' This shows how Caesar realised at once the danger which has been repeated throughout history.

18. **exirent.** Governed by *temperaturos quin*.

20. **Rhodanus.** Perhaps *solus* is omitted; the meaning in any case is ' *only* the Rhône . . . '

20. **quibus rebus.** Dative, with *occurendum*: ' he thought that he ought to meet these dangers . . . '

XXXIV

2, 3. **medium utriusque.** 'Half-way between (each of) them.'

3, 4. **re publica . . . rebus.** ' matters of state, vitally concerning . . . '

5. **esset.** Would still be this in direct speech; Ariovistus said ' *si quid mihi opus esset* (if I needed anything —but I *don't*—) *venissem* (I would have . . .) '. Thus, these are really ' vivid ' tenses, as is *velit*.

6. **ille.** Caesar : *se* : understand *facere*.

8. possideret. This, and the other subordinate verbs, are in the ' natural ' historic tenses.

11. quid. With *negoti* (partitive genitive, like *quid auxili* in ch. xxxi).

XXXV

All is Indirect Statement after *mittit*, explaining *mandatis*. Subordinate verbs are in ' natural ' historic tenses.

3, 4. in consulatu suo. The previous year, 59 B.C. See note on ch. xxxiii; probably this honour was given to Ariovistus to ensure his neutrality against the Helvetii; it cost nothing, apparently, but what had the Gauls thought about it?

2. quoniam. With *referret*, three lines below.

3. adfectus. Concessive : ' although . . . ', or ' after being . . . '

5. hanc gratiam. ' . . . such (a poor) return . . . '

11. redderet. Understand *ut*, containing the idea of ' command.'

16. M. Messalla M. Pisone consulibus.   61 B.C., as in ch. ii.

16, 17. censuisset. A regular technical term for a decree of the Senate; *decerno* and *placet* are also used. Caesar is showing his hand, and has put both the Senate and himself in the right, so far as the negotiations go.

18. commodo. Instrumental ablative : ' *with* benefit to . . . '

XXXVI

Again, all is Indirect Statement after *respondit*.

1–3. ius . . . imperarent. Take *imperarent* at once after *qui* (=*ei qui*) *vicissent*.

3. ad. ' in accordance with . . . '

6. **uteretur.** Virtually indirect command : ' how they should . . . '

10, 11. **qui suo adventu vectigalia sibi deteriora faceret.** *suo*=' his '—Caesar's, the subject of *faceret*, *sibi*—dative of ' disadvantage '; translate ' *his* tribute '— refers to Ariovistus, the ' subject ' of the whole passage of Indirect Statement.

Encouraged by Caesar's presence and success, the Aedui were stiffening their attitude towards Ariovistus.

12. **iniuria.** Instrumental abl., used as adverb.

14, 15. **longe his . . . a futurum.** ' Their title of Brothers of the Roman people would help them little ' (*lit.* be far from them).

15. **quod.** ' As to the fact that . . . '

17. **secum.** i.e. Ariovistus : *sua*—refers to *neminem.*

18. **congrederetur.** Command, ' let him . . . '

19. **annos XIIII.** Since 71 B.C.

XXXVII

1. **eodem tempore . . . et.** ' *Just as* this message . . . , envoys . . . . '

2. **questum.** Again, acc. of ' supine,' for purpose with ' motion.'

6. **Sueborum.** A great people, or group of peoples, of Northern Germany. Caesar describes them (book 4, ch. I) as ' by far the greatest and most warlike of all the Germans.' Things are becoming very serious; it seems that Ariovistus may be the ' spearhead ' for a general thrust to the west of the German peoples.

5, 6. **centum pagos.** A round figure : there were ' very many ' cantons (clans) of the Suebi. Caesar later (book 4, ch. i) speaks of the ' 100 cantons ' : here the Treveri are in terror speaking of ' the Suebi—all 100 cantons of them ! '

13. **ad.** ' to meet . . . '

XXXVIII

For the whole of the rest of the book, consult the map on page 42.

4. **tridui viam.**   Caesar probably started from Bibracte (where the Gallic chiefs met him), about 100 miles in a straight line from Vesontio, and many unsuccessful attempts have been made to trace his route.

3. **Vesontionem.**   Besançon, on the River *Dubis* (Doubs). See map on page 42 Ariovistus never reached it : Caesar did.

5. **id.** i.e., *ne occuparet Vesontionem.* Take this clause after *praecavendum* (understand *esse*).

7. **usui.** Dative of purpose, used predicatively.

7, 8. **natura loci.** ' site.'

11. **non amplius.** ' not more (than) . . . '—the usual way of saying this, as in English ' a thousand, not more.'

11, 12. **M sescentorum.** The manuscript omits M (1000), which was inserted (for accuracy) by the French Emperor Napoleon III.

12. **intermittit.** Intransitive.

13. **magna altitudine.** Abl. (' with ') of description, with *mons.*

XXXIX

1, 2. **rei frumentariae commeatusque causa.** (*a*) For the arrival of the supplies he had ordered (ch. xxxvii)—and to arrange for more from Vesontio itself, a rich town ; (*b*) to establish his lines of communication (*commeatus*=' comings-and-goings ').

3, 4. **ingenti magnitudine.** See *magna altitudine* (ch. xxxviii). What other words in this sentence are used in the same way ?

10. **tribunis militum.** Some of these would be inexperienced young men; see Introduction, pp. 16, 17.

10. **praefectis.** Commanders of the allied troops.

10. **reliquisque.** Some would be young aides-de-camp (*contubernales*), getting their first taste of war.

12, 13. **alius alia causa inlata.** abl. abs.; ' making different excuses.'

14. **diceret.** Not really in indirect statement, but attracted to the subjunctive (it often happens) because of the idea of reported speech.

14, 15. **non nulli.** As always, ' not a few.'

19, 20. **vulgo . . . obsignabantur.** Imagine Caesar smiling as he wrote this.

23. **qui.** Understand *ei*.

24. **non se hostem vereri, sed . . . .** Perhaps Caesar kept a straight face as he wrote *this*.

24. **angustias itineris.** Not as at the Pas de l'Ecluse, but other kinds of ' difficulties ' and hardships.

26. **ut.** With ' fearing ' verbs *ut* often=*ne non*.

28. **nuntiarant.** =*nuntiaverant*. *Not* ' announced.'

28, 29. **cum . . . iussisset.** Subjunctive in indirect statement: part of what they said to Caesar.

28. **signa ferri.** The regular phrase for an ' advance ' and for ' marching off.' The troops moved and fought in units, identified by their *signa*.

XL

For simple, straightforward narration of the ' background ' of the story, Caesar uses short, matter-of-fact chapters. A climax has now been reached; the morale of the army is breaking : Caesar says more. All is necessary, all is still straightforward and simple, but the dramatic effect is heightened.

After *primum*, the whole chapter is in Indirect Statement, till the last sentence.

5. **putarent.** Almost ' for daring to think . . . '

5. **se consule.** See note on ch. xxxv.

8. **persuaderi.** with acc. and inf.=' persuade *that* . . .'

11. **quod si.** there ' but if . . . '

12, 13. **sua**—*their* own; *ipsius*—*his* (own).

13. **factum.** *esse* understood.

13, 14. **periculum.** Not ' danger.'

14, 15. **Cimbris et Teutonis a C. Mario pulsis.** At the battles of Aquae Sextiae (Aix-en-Provence, 102 B.C.) and the Raudine Plains (in N. Italy, 101 B.C.). See the Index.

14–16. **cum . . . videbatur.** Not subjunctive (as subordinate verbs in indirect statement generally are), but indicative, because this simply means ' at the time when.' With this meaning, *cum* takes the indicative, and Caesar wishes to be absolutely clear. Do not translate ' *videbatur* ' by ' seemed.'

17. **servili tumultu.** In 73–71 B.C. there was in Italy a great rising of slaves, led by Spartacus. They beat several forces sent against them and were finally wiped out by Pompey. *Tumultus* was the regular word for a rising of this kind.

17. **tamen.** Adverb, not conjunction.

17. **aliquid.** Accusative of extent—' who, nevertheless, got *some* help from . . . '

19. **boni.** With ' *quantum*.'

20, 21. **quos . . . hos.** As so often in Latin, the relative comes first.

24, 25. superarint . . . potuerint. 'Vivid' tenses, introduced by the strong demonstrative *hos*.

26. adversum . . . Gallorum. Admagetobriga : see ch. xxxi.

29. sui potestatem fecisset. 'Given them the chance (to fight) him.'

31. ratione atque consilio. 'Well-thought-out tactics.' The Germans often showed themselves cunning fighters.

31–33. cui . . . hac. See note on '*quos . . . hos*' above. *Hac*, understand *ratione*.

37. sibi curae. See note on ch. xxxiii.

42. quibuscumque. *eis* understood, with *defuisse* and *convictam esse*. Say 'in the case of all those who . . . '

44–46. suam innocentiam perpetua vita esse perspectam. A large claim, and Caesar's troops knew exactly what Caesar meant; he had a sense of humour, several times exemplified in this passage.

49. pudor. Not quite 'shame'; a soldier's 'honour.'

51. decima legione. His best troops, now mentioned for the first time.

52. praetoriam cohortem. The commander-in-chief's bodyguard.

XLI

3. princeps decima legio. After what he had said about the Tenth, it was natural that they should come to him first.

7. primorum ordinum centurionibus. The *primipili*, or senior centurions in each legion.

7. egerunt uti. 'Came before Caesar to apologize . . . '

9. summa. A noun; look carefully in the vocabulary.

11. **ex aliis.** Used like *ceteris*: take closely with *maximam, fidem,* which we should rather make comparative, saying ' more . . . than the rest.'

12, 13. **ut . . . duceret.** Explains *exquisito itinere,* amounts to an instruction—'(who advised him) to lead . . .'

12, 13. **milium amplius quinquaginta.** Not, of course, the whole of his march from Vesontio, which took six to seven days (*septimo die,* below) of hard marching, but only the detour which he took to keep in open country (*locis apertis*), and avoid a possible ambush.

13, 14. **de quarta vigilia, ut dixerat.**   3–6 a.m. : he kept the promise, made in his address to the troops, to march ' before dawn.'

14, 15. **septimo die, cum iter non intermitteret.** No respite was given : not only did he wish to prevent Ariovistus from coming too far, but he wished to keep his troops occupied. The whole march was over 110 miles, in virtually unknown country. How widely his scouts operated is shown by the distance at which they located Ariovistus's forces—twenty-four (Roman) miles.

XLII

2, 3. **quod . . . postulasset, . . . id . . . fieri licere.** *quod* is *not* ' because '; it is ' as to the fact that . . .', but this would be awkward. Say ' his previous request . . . could now . . .' Perhaps Ariovistus wished to gain time; perhaps he really thought that ' the mountain was coming to Mahomet.'

8, 9. **fore uti . . . desisteret.** A normal roundabout way of expressing the future infinitive—simply ' he would . . .'

10. **quintus.** *Four* days later : see note on *in tertium annum* (Ch. iii).

10. **interim . . . cum legati.** Take *cum* first.

14. **veniret.** Command.

17, 18. **omnibus equis Gallis equitibus detractis.**
Gallis equitibus is dative ('person interested,' or 'disadvantage'), as usual with verbs of 'depriving'; the rest is ablative absolute; we would say '... to take away ... and mount ....'

18. **eo.** 'Thither'=on the horses.

25. **ad equum rescribere.** The regular phrase for entering the list of Knights—'to make one a Knight.' The *equites* (*ordo equester*) at Rome, originally those who could afford to keep a horse and serve in the cavalry in the old citizen-army, were now the class of 'big business,' led by Caesar's ally Crassus. Another joke.

XLIII

1. **planities.** The plain of Alsace.

1. **tumulus terrenus.** Perhaps an artificial mound or 'barrow,' but probably the conspicuous hill of Plettig.

6, 7. **ut ... ut.** Take before *ex equis* and *praeter se*.

8. **ventum est.** 'When *they* came'; like the French 'quand *on* y arriva,' or the English '*one* came.' Latin likes this 'impersonal' passive when the subject is vaguely expressed : cf. *pugnatum est*: 'there was a battle.'

11. **missa.** *essent* understood. *quod* is rather 'that' than 'because.'

11. **amplissime.** 'on a generous scale.'

13. **illum.** Ariovistus.

13, 14. **aditum ... haberet.** 'had no right to appear before the Senate, and no proper claim to these distinctions.'

14. **sua.** 'his own ...' (Caesar's).

16. **ipsis.** The Romans—dative of possession, with *intercederent*, 'existed between ...'

18. **ut.** 'how' (the first meaning).

22. **sui.** Partitive genitive of *suum*, with *nihil:* ' . . . of what was theirs.'

23, 24. **quod . . . id . . . quis.** Reverse the order: ' who could . . . what . . . '

24. **eis.** Dative: see note on *Gallis equitibus* (ch. xlii).

27. **redderet.** Command.

28. **at.** More of an adverb than a conjunction : ' at any rate.'

XLIV

The whole chapter is in Indirect Statement after *praedicavit*.

5, 6. **ipsis, ipsorum.** The *Gauls* themselves.

10. **uno proelio.** Admagetobriga (ch. xxxi).

12, 14. **velint . . . pependerint.** The Gauls; a veiled hint to Caesar not to interfere.

14, 15. **sibi ornamento et praesidio, non detrimento.** ' Predicative ' datives, with second dative (*sibi*) of ' person interested ' or ' recipient ': so we say ' . . . *for* a distinction ' etc.

19. **quod.** *Not* ' because ' : ' that,' ' granted that,' —' as to the fact that.'

20. **traducat.** It was still going on : see ch. xxxvii.

21. **nisi.** ' he had not come without being asked ' or positively ' he had come by invitation.' How often has this excuse been made by other invaders.

22. **defenderit.** Rather ' resisted attack ' (*bellum*).

24, 25. **numquam . . . egressum.** To be taken literally. There is no record that a Roman army *had* before operated outside the Province, and Ariovistus is telling Caesar to mind Rome's own business.

27. **ipsi.** Ariovistus : understand *sibi*.

30. **quod.** See note above, and choose carefully.

32. bello Allobrogum proximo. ' recent . . . ' : in 61 B.C. See note on ch. vi.

33. contentionibus. The quarrels between the Aedui and Sequani; and the troubles between the Gauls and Germans leading to Admagetobriga. Ariovistus was quite correct. All that Rome had done was to instruct the Roman governor (vaguely) to help Rome's allies 'if possible ' (ch. xxxv), and she *had* flirted with Ariovistus by giving him honours. Still, negotiations of this kind are hard, and what seems right one year is often proved wrong the next, particularly in dealing with aggressors, as modern history shows.

35. debere. ' He was forced to . . . '

36. quod. See above, and choose carefully. Translate *simulata amicitia* as a verb—' that Caesar had . . . and . . . ' —It is easy to understand Ariovistus's argument, and the fact that Caesar quotes it so fully suggests that his account of the interview is accurate.

37. qui. Used as conjunction: ' if he did not . . . '; *decedat*, and other verbs down to *interfecerit*, are vivid, for vivid threats.

39. quod si. Almost ' but if ' : better ' if, then, . . . '— *quod* is a conjunction—' with regard to this . . . ' Ariovistus is showing that he was *non imperitus rerum*—he knew the political situation at Rome.

45. praemio. From threats, Ariovistus moves to bribes; his language is less heated, and Caesar now uses historic tenses (*decessisset*, etc.).

45. quaecumque . . . confecturum. See Introduction, p. 9.

XLV

All this chapter, from *neque suam*, is in Indirect Statement.

1. in eam sententiam . . . quare. Together: (' to this effect, why ')—' to show why . . . '

4. esse. ' belonged to . . . '

5, 6. **Arvernos et Rutenos.** See the map on p. 42; and Introduction, p. 14. By this victory, the Romans secured their hold on the Province.

8. **quod.** Little more than a conjunction, and need not be translated : not ' *but* if.'

8. **antiquissimum quodque tempus.** ' Every historical precedent.' Ariovistus cannot select episodes to support his claims. If right of conquest was to be observed, the Romans had been in Gaul, as victors, long before Ariovistus and the Germans.

12. **voluisset.** The Senate.

XLVI

2. **propius.** Adverb, used rather like preposition, with *tumulum*—though it might be simply an adverb, in which case *accedere* would govern *tumulum* directly. Remember, though, that adverbs and prepositions are close relations. The Germans, less disciplined than the Romans, are growing impatient.

7. **committendum.** Understand *sibi esse*—' that he ought not to do anything . . . '. cf. ch. xiii, last sentence.

8. **per fidem.** Often used with verbs of ' deceiving ' —' through his (Ariovistus's) (misplaced) trust.' Almost ' treacherously ' (cf. *perfidus*, ' perfidious ').

11. **interdixisset.** *interdicere alicui* (*ab*) *aliqua re* = to forbid someone something.

12, 13. **eaque res . . . diremisset.** Take *ut* (=' how') first.

XLVII

1. **biduo post**=*postridie*. Why ? (See notes on ' *quintus* '—ch. xlii—and the other passage there quoted.)

3. **uti.** (=*ut*) : ' (*he asked*) that . . . ' Caesar often omits the *ut*.

5. **Caesari ... visa non est.** ' Caesar saw no ... ' : *videor* does not always mean ' seem.'

7. **e suis.** ' one of his own men ... '

7, 8. **magno cum periculo.** ' that it would be very dangerous for him to send.'

9, 10. **C. Valerium Procillum.** Mentioned also in ch. xix.

12. **civitate donatus erat.** When Valerius Flaccus was governor of the Province (83 B.C.), the citizenship had lately been given to many Italians (see Introduction, pp. 2–3). Others also received it.

12. **fidem.** *Caesar's* trust.

13, 14. **qua multa utebatur.** ' spoke fluently.'

12–14. **et ... et quod.** ' both ... and because ... ' *esset* subjunctive after *visum est; donatus erat* is an ordinary relative clause, not part of the indirect statement.

20. **an.** Introduces a violent rhetorical question : ' is it ... ? '

20. **prohibuit.** Not ' prevented ' : a stronger word.

XLVIII

2. **sub monte.** Almost certainly *Vosego* = the Vosges. Ariovistus chooses his ground cunningly. He wishes to cut Caesar's line of communication : the high ground of the Vosges gave him a safe line for his flank march. See plate VIII.

8, 9. **ut ... non deesset.** Purpose; *non deesset* form really one idea—' that ... might be not-lacking ' = ' to give A. every opportunity.' (Normally, negative purpose is introduced by *ne*, which would here give the wrong emphasis.)

11. **hoc.** Put last : ' as follows.'

14. **copia.** Here ' force '—(' supply ' of men).

16. **quid durius.** ' if they met difficulties.'

17. **qui.** adjective; understand *eques*.

17. **si . . . deciderat.** Frequentative : ' if ever . . . '—
cf. *cum* + pluperfect indicative—' whenever.'

19. **exercitatione.**   Ablative   of   cause — ' because
of . . . '

20. **sublevati.**   Imagine what happened; this is a
literal rendering of it. ' they could keep up with the
horses (*cursum adaequarent*) by holding on to the manes.'

LXIX

1, 2. **ne . . . prohiberetur.** This is the purpose of what
comes after. It looks as though Ariovistus might have
succeeded in his object, had Caesar not taken action.

4. **acieque triplici instructa.**   He   marched   in
battle order. See ch. xxiv.

6, 7. **hic locus . . . aberat.** Repeated (*ut dictum est*) to
stress the shortness of the distance—less than half-a-mile.
Caesar is both trying to restore his line of communication
(*ultra eum locum*, etc.), and trying to make the Germans
fight by ' trailing his coat.'

13. **legiones.** Altogether, six—remember, *one* originally
in the Province (chs. vii, viii), *three* from Aquileia
(ch. x), and *two* newly raised in Cisalpine Gaul (ch. x);
probably about 30,000 men, or rather fewer.   The
' *auxilia* ' may have numbered about 3,000; the cavalry
about 2,500.

14. **castra maiora.** The original camp, about two-and-
a-half-miles away.

L

3, 4. **hostibus . . . fecit.** ' offered battle.'

5. **circiter.**   Generally, an adverb; here, a preposition.

6, 7. **quae . . . oppugnaret.** Purpose. The battle was
drawn, but the camp was not taken.

13, 14. **sortibus et raticinationibus.** The Roman historian Tacitus, writing about 150 years later, says that the Germans used 'soothsaying' and 'divination' as much as any people, and describes a method of fortune-telling by slips of wood.

15. **non esse fas.** 'It was not the will of the gods.'

16. **novam lunam.** This 'new moon' (with the statement about the crops in ch. xl) can be exactly fixed as that of September 18th, 58 B.C.

LI

2. **alarios** = *auxilia*—posted on the wings (*alae*).

4. **pro.** 'compared with.'

5. **ad speciem.** To put up a better appearance : 'to impress (the enemy).'

7, 8. **necessario . . . eduxerunt.** Make *necessario* the verb : 'were forced to . . .'

10, 11. **raedis et carris.** *raeda*—a large four-wheeled cart like the 'covered wagon' of the American and South African pioneers; *carrus*, a two-wheeled vehicle like a farm-cart.

12. **eo.** (thither): 'in the carts.'

LII

1, 2. **quaestorem.** The word means 'inspector' or 'supervisor.' There were civilian 'quaestors' at Rome, who were largely financial officers; in the provinces, quaestors had administrative duties; in war, they might be quartermasters, supply officers, or (as here) employed in fighting.

2. **testis virtutis.** It was a great encouragement to the men to know that their superior officers would see how they fought.

4, 6. **ita . . . ita.** With *acriter* and *repente*.

7. **pila . . . coiciendi.** The regular way of beginning
a battle: the heavy *pila* (see ch. xxv) cast the enemy
into confusion. So modern armies use artillery and small
arms' fire before an attack.

7. **reiectis.** ' dropped '—*very* quickly; time was short.

8. **gladiis.** The usual second stage. The short *gladius*
was used for stabbing, not cutting and slashing.

9. **phalange facta.** See ch. xxiv, and note. The
Germans were fond of fighting in large masses, and
sometimes fought chained together.

11. **in phalangas.** Greek acc. pl. The legionaries
jumped on the locked shields (ch. xxiv, note).

11. **qui insilirent . . . revellerent . . . vulnerarent.**
Like *sunt qui* with subjunctive—really ' result.'

12, 13. **a sinistro cornu.** That first attacked, by the
Roman *right* (see above).

15, 16. **P. Crassus adulescens.** *Adulescens*, probably a
straightforward   adjective   of   description—' young '
Crassus—not an attempt to distinguish him from his
father or brother.

16. **expeditior.** The *tertia acies;* this clause (*quod . . .
versabantur*) should come last.

It is clear from the last sentence that Caesar himself
was heavily engaged elsewhere, probably on the Roman
right, when this crucial moment arrived; and he gives
' young Crassus ' all the credit for his decisive action.

18. **laborantibus nostris.** See vocabulary; dative of
advantage. *subsidio:* dative of purpose.

LIII

1, 2. **terga verterunt.** This was often the end of an
ancient battle; after a ferocious hand-to-hand struggle,
sometimes very short, one side would be seized with panic

and bolt. Less disciplined peoples were particularly liable to do this; the more civilised Romans generally endured better.

How the Germans escaped when the way to safety was blocked by their wagons Caesar does not say. Frontinus (over a century after) says that the Germans, hemmed in, were fighting desperately, and that Caesar ordered them to be given a way out, to make the rout easier.

2–4. **neque prius destiterunt . . . pervenerunt.** The manuscripts all say *quinque* or ' V '; three other historians —Plutarch, Orosius, and Eutropius—all say fifty. Five miles is much too little, unless (which is not very likely) Caesar confused the river Ill (*Helella*) with the main stream of the Rhine; fifty miles is much too far, for the Rhine was nearer than that, nor could any army continue its flight so far without stopping. Therefore *quindecim* is suggested.

8. **interfecerunt.** Ruthless, but decisive; the Germans did not trouble Caesar again for some time.

13. **trinis.** Distributive : *all* his chains (pl.) were triple. Three is a ' magic ' number, and Procillus was to be sacrificed.

21. **is.** Procillus : *se praesente*, abl. abs., closely with *consultum* (*esse*, understood).

21. **ter.** Magic : see note on *trinis*, above.

LIV

3. **Ubii.** The German tribes were constantly quarrelling, and the Ubii seized their chance to fall on their rivals.

6. **maturius.** To emphasize that he *had* finished the year's campaigns; but also, because his troops were tired.

7. **in Sequanos.** He did not return to the Province; more will be done later, and the Roman claim is stated.

8. **citeriorem Galliam.** Cisalpine Gaul.

8. **conventus.** Caesar was civil, as well as military governor; these were ' regional assemblies,' or we might say ' assizes,' though other work beside legal would be done. Caesar generally spent the winter in Northern Italy. It was nearer Rome, where much that affected his interests was happening.

INDEX OF PROPER NAMES

(*N.B.* When a man has more than one name, look up his last name.)

Admagetobriga, -ae (*f,*): the scene of Ariovistus's defeat of the Gauls in 61 B.C., probably on the upper Saône. See the note on ch. xxxi.

Aedui, -orum (*m.*): a powerful Celtic people of Central Gaul, between the Loire (*Liger*) and Saône, rivals of the Arverni and Sequani; loyal allies of Rome since 121 B.C.; defeated by Ariovistus and the Germans, 61 B.C.

Aemilus, Lucius: a subordinate officer (decurion) of Gallic cavalry.

Allobroges, -um (*m.*): a Gallic tribe between the Isère (*Isara*) and Rhône; they were restive, and (61 B.C.) rose, but were put down.

Alpes, -ium (*f.*): the Alps.

Ambarri, -ovum (*m.*): a tribe of Central Gaul, East of the Saône, near Maçon (Matisco), related to the Aedui.

Aquileia, -ae (*f.*): an important town at the head of the Adriatic. The Romans established it as an outpost in 182 B.C. In 58 B.C. most of Caesar's force (3 legions) was quartered there. Destroyed by Attila the Hun in 452 A.D., its inhabitants afterwards founded Venice, on the nearby lagoons.

Aquitani, -orum (*m.*): a people partly Gallic, partly Iberian, living in *Aquitania* (Aquitaine), between the river Garonne and the Pyrenees.

Aquitania, -ae (*f.*): see **Aquitani.**

Arar (or Araris), -is (*m.*): the river Saône.

Ariovistus, -i (*m.*): German chieftain who, in 71 B.C., entered Gaul at the invitation of the Sequani and Arverni, to help them against the Aedui, but behaved so high-handedly that the three tribes turned against him, only to be badly beaten (see **Admagetobriga**). Driven from Gaul by Caesar and died soon after.

Arverni, -orum (*m.*): a very powerful Gallic tribe, in the Auvergne; allies of the Sequani and rivals of the Aedui; beaten by Q. Fabius Maximus in 121 B.C.; in or after 71 B.C., called in Ariovistus and the Germans to their aid against the Aedui, with evil results. In 52 B.C., under Vercingetorix, they headed the last desperate rising against Caesar.

Belgae, -arum (*m.*): a warlike people, of mixed German and Celtic origin, between the rivers Marne, Seine, and Rhine. Came to Gaul in the 2nd century B.C., and to S.E. Britain in the 1st century B.C.

Bibracte, -is (*n.*): the chief town of the Aeduans, a place of considerable wealth and culture; now Mount Beauvray.

Bituriges, -um (*m.*): a powerful people of Central Gaul, in the loop of the Loire (Liger). Their chief town was Avaricum (now Bourges).

Boii, -orum (*m.*): a warlike and restless Gallic tribe, first formed in Central Gaul. Constantly on the move; some settled in N. Italy about 390 B.C. Others (of whom those mentioned were a part) moved Eastwards, and later gave their name to Bohemia. Under pressure from the Dacians of Roumania, they joined the Helvetii.

Caburus, Gaius Valerius: a Gaul, father of C. Valerius Procillus (see below): loyal to Rome, and, like many others, granted Roman citizenship, taking the name of his patron (see **Flaccus**).

Caesar, Gaius Julius: see Introduction.

Cassius, Lucius: consul in 107 B.C., defeated and killed by the Helvetians (**Tigurini**), who were marching with the **Cimbri**.

Casticus, -i (*m.*): a Sequanian noble, who plotted with **Orgetorix.**

Catamantaloedes, -is (*m.*): a Sequanian noble, father of **Casticus**; chief of his people for many years, and honoured by Rome.

Caturiges, -um (*m.*): a Ligurian Alpine tribe near Briançon (*Brigantio*), in the upper valley of the Durance (*Druentia*), hostile to the Romans.

Celtae, -arum (*m.*): the Celts originally lived in the upper valley of the Danube. They migrated in various directions —into Italy, into Greece, and into Asia Minor, where the Galatians of the New Testament were their descendants. Especially they moved Westwards, settling in Gaul, Britain, and Northern Spain.

Ceutrones, -um (*m.*): an Alpine Gallic tribe, in Savoy, hostile to the Romans: their chief town, Darantasia, is now Centron.

Cimberius, -ii (*m.*): a German chief, a leader of the **Suebi** and brother of **Nasua.**

Cimbri, -orum (*m.*): a powerful Celtic people, from Jutland. With the **Teutoni** they migrated South and West, and between 113 and 101 B.C. caused great loss and anxiety to Rome. Instead of entering Italy, they marched into Spain but returned in 102. Marius beat the Teutoni at Aquae Sextiae (Aix-en-Provence), and, the next year, beat the Cimbri at the Raudine Fields, near Verona.

Considius, Publius: an experienced officer in Caesar's army.

Crassus, Marcus Licinius: the great financier, politician, leader of the ' equestrian ' (business) party, and distinguished soldier.

Crassus, Publius Licinius: son of the above. Won distinction under Caesar; in 56 B.C., subdued Aquitania: went to the East with his father, and fell at Carrhae 53 B.C., where his father was beaten by the Parthians.

Diviciacus, -i: the Druid, a leader of the Aedui, and elder brother of **Dumnorix.** Visited Rome some years before to ask for help against the Sequani, and to buttress his own power against the rising influence of Dumnorix. He continued loyal to Rome throughout.

Divico, -onis: a Helvetian chief, leader of the **Tigurini** (107 B.C.) when they defeated **Cassius:** now again, 49 years later, comes as head of the Helvetian delegation to Caesar after his rout of the Tigurini.

Dubis, -is (*m.*)**:** the river Doubs.

Dumnorix, -igis: an Aeduan noble, younger brother of **Diviciacus:** married the daughter of **Orgetorix**, with whom, and with **Casticus,** he plotted to seize an empire

in Gaul. An enemy of Rome, and a constant thorn in Caesar's flesh. To keep him out of trouble, he was ordered to go with Caesar to Britain (54 B.C.): tried to escape, and was killed.

Flaccus, Gaius Valerius: Governor of the Province in 83 B.C.

Gabinius, Aulus: consul in 58 B.C.; afterwards served with Caesar in the Civil War against Pompey and the Senatorial party.

Galli, -orum (*m.*)**:** see **Gallia,** and **Celtae.**

Gallia, -ae (*f.*)**:** (i) Gaul—*i.e.,* roughly, France: the whole of the area inhabited by the **Galli** (Gauls) and kindred peoples, shortly described by Caesar in ch. i.
(ii) One or other of the Gallic provinces already established in 58 B.C., when Caesar became governor: *viz.* ' Hither ' or ' Further ' Gaul (the Province).

Garumna, -ae (*f.*)**:** the river Garonne.

Genava, -ae (*f.*)**:** Geneva; then an important town of the Allobroges.

Germani, -orum (*m.*)**:** this name was given to many tribes and peoples, living, roughly, between the Danube (Danuvius or Hister), the Rhine, the North Sea (Mare Germanicum) and the Baltic (Mare Suebicum—see **Suebi**) —*i.e.,* more or less, modern Germany.

Graioceli, -orum (*m.*): an Alpine Gallic tribe, near Mont Cénis, hostile to the Romans.

Harudes, -um (*m.*): a German tribe on the upper Danube, who in 58 began to cross the Rhine to join Ariovistus in Alsace.

Helvetii, -orum (*m.*): a Celtic people, occupying much of Switzerland (see ch. ii).

Hispania, -ae (*f.*): Spain; largely conquered by the Romans in the 2nd century B.C., and in Caesar's time governed by them in two provinces—Hispania Citerior (' hither ' or Northern), and Ulterior (' further ' or Southern.)

Italia, -ae: Italy—the modern Italy, without the wide northern plain of the Po.

Iura, -ae (*m.*): the Jura mountains.

Labienus, Titus Attius: ' legatus,' and second-in-command, with the rank of propraetor. He remained with Caesar throughout the wars in Gaul, and won great distinction. When the Civil War broke out in 49 B.C., he went over to Pompey's side (Caesar sending his baggage after him), and was killed at the battle of Munda, in Spain (45 B.C.), which ended the war.

Latovici, -orum (*m.*): a Celtic people, on the Austrian/Swiss frontier, East of the Helvetians, whose march they joined.

Lemannus lacus (*m.*): Lake Geneva, still called also Lake Leman.

Leuci, -orum (*m.*): a people of Gallia Belgica, on the upper Moselle (Mosella).

Lingones, -um (*m.*): an important people of Central Gaul, their capital, Andematurinum, was also called Lingones (Langres).

Liscus, -i: an Aeduan noble, who was Vergobret (below) in 58 B.C.

Marcomani, -orum (*m.*): a German tribe, who followed Ariovistus: later settled in Bohemia.

Marius, Gaius: the great Roman soldier and democratic statesman (157-86 B.C.)

Matrona, -ae (*f.*): the river Marne.

Maximus, Quintus Fabius: consul in 121 B.C.; beat the **Arverni** and **Ruteni** at the point where the Isère joins the Rhône. This victory sealed the future of the Roman province. Afterwards, he and his descendants became patrons of the Allobroges, with the title of 'Allobrogicus.'

Messalla, Marcus Valerius: consul in 61 B.C.

Mettius, Marcus: a Gaul, loyal to Rome: a close friend of the German chief, Ariovistus.

Nammeius, -ī: a Helvetian chief.

Nasua, -ae (*m.*): a German chief, a leader of the **Suebi** (see **Cimberius**).

Nemetes, -um (*m.*): a German tribe, in Alsace, opposite Strasbourg; followed Ariovistus.

Noreia, -ae (*f.*): a town in Noricum now (probably) Newmarkt.

Noricum, -ī (*n.*): part of Austria, between Vienna (Vindobona), the Danube, the Inn (Aunus), and the Alps: later, a Roman province.

Oceanus, -ī (*m.*): the Atlantic.

Ocelum, -ī (*n.*): a town of Cisalpine Gaul, on the Ligurian frontier; now probably Drubiaglio.

Orgetorix, -igis (*m.*): a great, powerful, and ambitious Helvetian noble. His story Caesar tells in chs. ii–iv.

Piso, Lucius Calpurnius: consul in 112 B.C.: second-in-command to **Cassius** (above) against the **Tigurini**, and killed in the rout. Also grandson of the above; consul in 58 B.C., with **Gabinius.** Caesar in 59 B.C. married his daughter, Calpurnia.

Piso, Marcus (Pupius): consul in 61 B.C., with **Messalla.**

Procillus, Gaius Valerius: a prominent Gaul of the Province, much trusted by Caesar, and employed by him as interpreter and confidential agent: son of **Caburus.**

Provincia, -ae (*f.*): see **Gallia** —the 'Province.'

Pyrenaei montes (*m.*): the Pyrenees.

Raurici, -orum: a Gallic people, near Basilea (Basle), on the Rhine: many of them joined the Helvetians, their neighbours.

Rhenus, -i (*m.*): the river Rhine.

Rhodanus, -i (*m.*): the river Rhône.

Ruteni, -orum (*m.*): a people of Aquitania, in the Tarnis (Tarn) valley.

Santones, -um (or -i, -orum, *m.*): a powerful people in Western Gaul, on the Bay of Biscay, North of the Garonne.

Sedusii, -orum (*m.*): a German tribe, South of the river Main: followed Ariovistus.

Segusiavi, -orum (*m.*): a tribe of Central Gaul, N.W. of Lugdunum (Lyon), just outside the Province.

Sequana, -ae (*f.*): the river Seine.

Sequani, -orum (*m.*): a very important tribe of Eastern Gaul, living roughly between the Saône, the Rhine, and Mount Jura; allies of the **Arverni** against the **Aedui,** and called in **Ariovistus.**

Suebi, -orum (*m.*): a name given to many German peoples, in many parts of Germany. They were said by the Treveri to have 'a hundred cantons'.

Sulla, Lucius Cornelius: 138-78 B.C.: the great soldier, dictator (82-79 B.C.), and senatorial champion.

Teutoni, -orum (also -is, -um) (*m.*): a powerful German people, from Schleswig-Holstein or the South Baltic, who joined the **Cimbri** in their march.

Tigurini, -orum (*m.*): one of the four cantons of the Helvetii, probably living near Zürich.

Tolosates, -ium (*m.*): a Gallic people near Tolosa (Toulouse), an important city on the Garonne.

Treveri, -orum (*m.*): a powerful people of Gallia Belgica, on the Moselle, partly German, partly Celtic; their chief city—later Augusta Treverorum—is now Trèves.

Triboces, -um (*m.*): a German people, between **Mons Vosegus** (Vosges) and the Rhine: followed Ariovistus.

Tulingi, -orum (*m.*): a Celtic or German people, living probably just East of the Upper Rhine: near neighbours of the Helvetians, whom they joined in their migration.

Ubii, -orum (*m.*): a German people, near Cologne.

Vangiones, -um: a German people, on the Rhine, south of Moguntiacum (Mainz): followed Ariovistus.

Verbigenus, -i (*m. adj.*): V. pagus, one of the four cantons of the Helvetii.

Vergobretus, -i (*m.*): the chief magistrate of the Aedui, elected annually.

Verucloetius, -ii (*m.*): a Helvetian chief, who negotiated with Caesar.

Vesontio, -onis (*m.*): the chief town of the **Sequani,** now Besançon, on the Doubs **(Dubis).**

Voccio, -onis (*m.*): a Norican chieftain, whose daughter married **Ariovistus.**

Vocontii, -orum (*m.*): a Gallic Alpine tribe of the Eastern Province, between the Isère (Isara) and Durance (Druentia): (modern Vaison).

VOCABULARY

(*N.B.* Only naturally long vowels are marked.)

A.: Aulus (Roman *praenomen*).

ā, ab (*prep.* with *abl.*): from, by, on the side of; in, among; **a dextro cornu:** on the right wing.

abdō, -dere, -didī, -ditum (*v.t.*): to hide.

abducō, -ere, -duxī, -ductum (*v.t.*): to take away, carry off.

absens, -ntis (*pr. part* of **absum**): absent, away.

abstineō, -ēre, -uī, -tentum (*v.i.*): to abstain from.

absum, abesse, āfuī (*v.i.*): to be absent, to be (so far) away from; **longe eis afuturum:** would help them little.

āc (*conj.*): and (emphatic), and moreover.

accēdō, -ere, -cessī, -cessum (*v.i.*): to approach; — **ad,** to reach; — **ad,** to be added to.

acceptus, -a, -um (*pfct. part. pass.* of **accipio**): popular.

accersō = arcessō.

accidō, -ere, -cidī (*v.i.*): to happen.

accipiō, -ere, -cēpī, -ceptum (*v.t.*): to receive; **accipere in deditionem:** to receive the surrender (of).

accurrō, -ere, -currī, -cursum (*v.i.*): to hurry up to.

accusō, -āre, -avi, -ātum (*v.t.*): to accuse, blame.

aciēs, -ēī (*f*): line of battle, army drawn up for battle (*cf.* **agmen:** army in line of march). **acies oculorum:** fierce gaze.

ācriter, ācrius, ācerrime (*adv.*): eagerly, vigorously.

ad (*prep.* with *acc.*): to, towards, up to, near, at, in accordance with; for, for the purpose of; (with numbers) up to (the number of), about. **ad multam noctem:** till late in the night.

adaequō, -āre, -āvī, -ātum (*v.t.*): to make equal to, to equal.

adamō, -āre, -āvī, -ātum (*v.t.*): to become very fond of.

addūcō, -ere, -xī, -ctum (*v.t.*): to bring, lead to, induce, influence.

adequitō, -āre, -āvī, -atum (*v.i.*): to ride towards.

adferō, -ferre, -tulī, -latum (*v.t.*): to bring, provide; (= **afferō**).

adficiō, -ere, -fēcī, -fectum (*v.t.*): to affect; **dolore adfici:** to be grieved, chagrined; **supplicio adficere:** to punish (= **afficiō**).

adfinitās, -ātis (*f.*): relationship, kinship (= **affinitās**).

adhibeō, -ēre, -uī, -itum (*v.t.*): to call in, consult.

aditus, -ūs (*m.*): access, right of approach, audience (with somebody).

admiror, -ārī, -ātus sum (*v.t.*): to wonder, be surprised at, admire.

admittō, -ere, -mīsī, -missum (*v.t.*): to let go; **equo admisso**: at full gallop.

adorior, -orīrī, -ortus sum (*v.t.*): to attack.

adscīscō, -ere, -scīvī, -scītum (*v.t.*): to admit, acknowledge as, receive.

adsum, -esse, adfuī (*v.i.*): to be present, to be ready.

adulescens, -ntis (*m.*, or *adj.*): young man, young.

adulescentia, -ae (*f.*): youth.

adventus, -ūs (*m.*): arrival.

adversus, -a, -um (*perf. pass. part.* of **adverto**): unfavourable; **adversum proelium**: defeat.

advertō, -ere, -tī, -versum (*v.t.*): to turn towards; **animum adverto**: to notice (= **animadverto**).

aedificium, -iī (*n.*): building, house.

aegrē, aegrius, aegerrimē (*adv.*): with difficulty.

aequitās, -ātis (*f.*): fairness.

aequō, -āre, -āvī, -ātum (*v.t.*): make equal.

aequus, -a, -um: equal, level, advantageous.

aestas, -ātis (*f.*): summer.

ager, agrī (*m.*): field, land; (*often in pl.*): land, territory.

aggredior, -ī, -gressus sum (*v.t.*): to attack.

agmen, -inis (*n.*): column, army; **agmen claudere**: to bring up the rear; **novissimo agmine**: in the rear.

agō, agere, ēgī, actum (*v.t.*, sometimes *v.i.*): to perform, do, deal (with someone); hold (a meeting, etc.); **gratias agere**: to thank.

alacritās, -ātis (*f.*): eagerness, enthusiasm.

ālārius, -a, -um: auxiliary; **alāriī, -orum**: auxiliary troops (*cf.* **auxilia**).

aliēnus, -a, -um: unfavourable.

aliquamdiu (*adv.*): for a considerable time.

aliquis, -quid (*indef. pron.*): someone, some; **aliquid**: to some extent.

alius, -a, -ud: other, another; **alius alia causa illata**: each making a different excuse, making various excuses.

alō, -ere, aluī, altum (*v.t.*): to maintain, keep, support.

alter, -a, -um (*pron.* or *adj.*): the one (or) the other (of two): the second; another; anyone else; **alteri ... alteri**: the one party . . . the other (party) . . .

altitūdō, -dinis (*f.*): height, depth.

altus, -a, -um: high, deep.

āmentia, -ae (*f.*): folly, madness.

amīcitia, -ae (*f.*): friendship.

amīcus, -i (*m.*): friend; as *adj.*: friendly.

āmittō, -ere, -mīsī, -missum (*v.t.*): to lose, destroy.

amor, -ōris (*m.*): love.

amplē, amplius, amplissimē (*adv.*): generously.

amplius (*adv.*): more, more than.

an (*conj.*): or; **an speculandī causā**: was it to spy? (indignant question).

anceps, -cipitis (*adj.*): doubtful, indecisive.

angustiae, -ārum (*f.*): difficulty, pass (through mountains).

angustus, -a, -um: narrow, restricted.

animadvertō, -ere, -tī, -sum (*v.t.*): to notice; **animadvertere in** and *acc.*, to punish (same as **animum adverto**).

animus, -i (*m.*): mind, heart, spirit, sympathy, feelings; in *pl.*, courage; **bono animo esse in** and *acc.*, to be friendly towards.

annus, -i (*m.*): year.

annuus, -a, -um: yearly.

ante (*prep.* with *acc.*): before, in front of.

ante, anteā (*adv.*): before, beforehand.

antīquus, -a, -um: old, former, ancient.

aperiō, -īre, -uī, -tum (*v.t.*): to open.

apertus, -a, -um: open, unprotected (*perf. pass. part.* of **aperio**).

appellō, -āre, -āvī, -ātum (*v.t.*): to call.

appetō, -ere, -īvī, -ītum (*v.t.*): to seek, strive for.

Aprīlis, -e: of April (often abbreviated to Apr.).

apud (*prep.* with *acc.*): among, in presence of, with, in the hands of.

arbitrium, -iī (*n.*): will, judgment.

arbitror, -ārī, -ātus sum (*v.i.*): to think, consider.

arcessō, -ere, -īvī, -ītum (*v.t.*): to send for, summon, call (same as **accerso**).

arma, -orum (*n. pl.*): arms, force of arms.

arroganter, -ius, -issimē (*adv.*): proudly, haughtily, selfishly, impudently.

arrogantia, -ae (*f.*): pride, haughtiness.

arx, arcis (*f.*): citadel, stronghold.

ascendō, -ere, -dī, -sum (*v.t.*): to climb, ascend.

ascensus, -ūs (*m.*): ascent, way up.

at (*conj.*): but, at any rate.

atque, āc (*conj.*): and (emphatic), moreover; **par . . . atque**: the same . . . as.

attingō, -ere, -tigī, -tactum (*v.t.*): to reach, border on.

auctoritās, -ātis (*f.*): influence.

audācia, -ae (*f.*): boldness.

audacter, -ius, -issimē (*adv.*): boldly.

audeō, -ēre, ausus sum (*v.i.*): to dare.

audiō, -īre, -īvī, -ītum (*v.t.*): hear, listen to; **dicto audiens**: obedient.

augeō, -ēre, auxī, auctum (*v.t.*): to increase.

aut (*conj.*): or; **aut . . . aut**: either . . . or.

autem (*conj.*): but, however, moreover, whereas.

auxilia, -ōrum (*n. pl.*): auxiliary troops, allied troops (*cf.* **alarii**).

auxilium, -iī (*n.*): aid.

avāritia, -ae (*f.*): greed; corruption, dishonesty.

āversus, -a, -um (*perf. pass. part.* of **averto**): turned in flight, fleeing.

āvertō, -ere, -tī, -sum (*v.t.*): to divert, turn away; **animum avertere**: to estrange.

avus, -ī (*m.*): grandfather.

barbarus, -a, -um: barbarous, savage. As *noun*, **barbarī, -ōrum** (*m.*): barbarians.

bellicōsus, -a, -um: warlike.

bellō, -āre, -āvī, -ātum (*v.i.*): to make war, fight.

bellum, -ī (*n.*): war; **bellum inferō**: to make war on, invade.

beneficium, -iī (*n.*): benefit, favour, kindness, lucky turn; **beneficio** and *gen.*, thanks to . . . ; **beneficio obstringo**: to put under an obligation.

bīduum, -ī (*n.*): (period of) two days.

biennium, -iī (*n.*): (period of) two years.

bipertītō (*adv.*): in two divisions.

bonitās, -ātis (*f.*): excellence, goodness.

bonum, -ī (*n.* of *bonus*, used as *noun*): good, benefit; **bono animo esse in** and *acc.*: to be friendly to, well-disposed towards . . .

bonus, -a, -um: good.

bracchium, -iī (*n.*): arm.

brevis, -e: short.

C: centum: 100.

C.: Gaius (Roman *praenomen*).

cadō, -ere, cecidī, cāsum (*v.i.*): to fall, to be killed.

calamitās, -ātis (*f.*): defeat, disaster, mishap.

capiō, -ere, cēpī, captum (*v.t.*): to take, capture, receive, win, catch off one's guard; **initium capio**: to begin.

captīvus, -i (*m.*): prisoner.

caput, -itis (*n.*): head, human being.

carrus, -ī (*m.*): cart.

castellum, -ī (*n.*): fort, strongpoint,

castra, -ōrum (*n. pl.*): camp; **castra moveo**: to strike camp, to shift camp.

cāsus, -ūs (*m.*): accident.

catēna, -ae (*f.*): chain.

causa, -ae (*f.*): cause, reason, case; **causam dico**: to plead one's case; **causā** (*abl.*): for the sake of, because of; **causam inferō**: to put forward a reason.

caveō, -ēre, cāvī, cautum (*v.i.*): to take care.

celeritās, -ātis (*f.*): speed.

celeriter, celerius, celerrimē (*adv.*): quickly.

censeō, -ēre, -uī, censum (*v.i.*): to decide, to decree (of the Senate).

census, -ūs (*m.*): count.

centum (*num.*): a hundred.

centuriō, -ōnis (*m.*): centurion; **centurio primi ordinis**: senior centurion.

certior fiō: to be informed, to learn (to be made more certain). Active form, **certiorem facio**: to inform.

certus, -a, -um: certain, fixed.

cēterī, -ae, -a (*pron.* or *adj.*): the others, the other.

cibāria, -ōrum (*n. pl.*): grain, provisions.

cingō, ere, -nxī, -nctum (*v.t.*): to surround.

circinus, -i (*m.*): pair of compasses.

circiter(*prep.* with *acc.*): about.

circuitus, -ūs (*m.*): circumference, circuit, detour; **in circuitu**: on different sides, all round.

circum (*prep.* with *acc.*): around, near.

circumdō, -dare, -dedī, -datum (*v.t.*): to surround, to build . . . round.

circumdūcō, -ere, -xī, -ctum (*v.t.*): to draw round.

circumsistō, -ere, -stitī (*v.i.*): to surround, to stand round.

circumveniō, -īre, -vēnī, -ventum (*v.t.*): to surround, to deceive.

citerior, -ius (*comp. adj.*, from **citra**): nearer, inner.

citrā (*prep.* with *acc.*): on the nearer side of.

citrō (*adv.*): hither; **ultro citroque**: hither and thither, backwards and forwards.

cīvitās, -ātis (*f.*): state, tribe.

claudō, -ere, -sī, -sum (*v.t.*): to close, to shut in; **claudo agmen**: to bring up the rear (of the column).

cliens, -ntis (*m.*): dependant.

coëmō, -ere, -ēmī, -emptum (*v.t.*): to buy up.

coepī, -isse, -ptum (*v.i.* with *infinitive*): to begin.

coerceō, -ēre, -uī, -itum (*v.t.*): to restrain.

cōgitō, -āre, -āvī, -atum (*v.t.*): to think, to consider, to wonder.

cognoscō, -ere, -nōvī, -nitum (*v.t.*): to get to know, to find out, to learn, to discuss, to examine; **cognovi** (*perfect* with *present* meaning):

to know; **cognosco causam**: to hear a case, to try a case.

cōgō, -ere, coēgī, coactum (*v.t.*): to bring together, gather; to compel.

cohors, -rtis (*f.*): cohort.

cohortor, -ārī, -ātus sum (*v.t.*): to encourage.

coiciō, -ere, coniēcī, -iectum (*v.t.*): to throw.

colligō, -āre, -āvī, -ātum (*v.t.*): to fasten together.

collis, -is (*m.*): hill.

collocō, -āre, -āvī, -ātum (*v.t.*): to establish, place : to give in marriage (see **nubo**).

colloquium, -ī (*n.*): parley.

colloquor, -ī, -locūtus sum (*v.i.*): to talk with, parley.

combūrō, -ere, -bussī, -bustum (*v.t.*): to burn.

commeatus, -ūs (*m.*): supplies, line of communication.

commemorō, -āre, -āvī, ātum (*v.t.*): to call to mind, speak of, mention.

commeō, -āre, -āvī, -ātum (*v.i.*): to come and go, to visit.

comminus (*adv.*): at close quarters, hand-to-hand.

committō, -ere, -mīsī, -missum (*v.t.*): to bring together; to entrust, to commit; **committo ut**: so to act . . . that . . . ; **committo proelium**: to join battle.

commodē, -ius, -issimē (*adv.*): conveniently, suitably, easily, well.

commodum, -ī (*n.*): benefit, advantage (*n.* of **commodus**).

commodus, -a, -um: suitable.

commonefaciō, -ere, -fēcī, factum (*v.t.*): to remind.

commoveō, -ēre, -mōvī, -mōtum (v.t.): to alarm, disturb, influence.

commūniō, -īre, -īvī, -ītum (v.t.): to fortify, to build (a fort, etc.).

commūnis, -e: common, general, affecting both sides.

commūtātio, -ōnis (f.): change, alteration.

commūtō, -āre, -āvī, -atum (v.t.): to change.

comparō, -āre, -āvī, -ātum (v.t.): to prepare; to collect; to get; to compare.

comperiō, -īre, -ī, -tum (v.t.): to find out, learn; compertum habeō: to know for certain.

complector, -ī, -plexus sum (v.t.): to embrace.

compleō, -ēre, -ēvī, -ētum (v.t.): to fill, cover.

complūrēs, -ium: several, a large number (of).

comportō, -āre, -āvī, ātum (v.t.): to bring together, collect.

conāta, -ōrum (n. pl.): enterprise.

conātus, -ūs (m.): attempt.

concēdō, -ere, -cessī, -cessum (v.i.): to yield; to grant a request, allow.

concīdō, -ere, -īdī, -īsum (v.t.): to cut to pieces, kill.

conciliō, -āre, -āvī, -ātum (v.t.): to win over.

concilium, -iī (n.): council, meeting.

conclāmō, -āre, -āvī, -ātum (v.i.): to shout, cry out.

concurrō, -ere, -currī, -cursum (v.i.): to rally, come to help.

concursus, -ūs (m.): gathering, concentration.

condiciō, -ōnis (f.): condition, offer, proposition; (pl.): terms.

condōnō, -āre, -āvī, -ātum (v.t.): to forgive, overlook.

condūcō, -ere, -xī, -ctum (v.t.): to gather, bring together.

conferō, -ferre, -tulī, -lātum (v.t.): to bring together, to collect; to compare; to postpone; to attribute to; conferre se: to go.

confertus, -a, -um: closely packed.

conficiō, -ere, -fēcī, -fectum (v.t.): to finish, complete; to compose, write; to draw up.

confīdō, -fīdere, -fīsus sum (v.i.): to be sure; to trust (with dat.).

confirmō, -āre, -āvī, -ātum (v.t.): to strengthen, assure; to settle; to declare.

congredior, -ī, -gressus sum (v.i.): to meet; to fight (with).

coniciō, -ere, -iēcī, -iectum: same as coicio.

coniungō, -ere, -iunxī, iunctum (v.t.): to join.

coniūrātio, -onis (f.): conspiracy, plot.

cōnor, -ārī, -ātus sum (v.i.): to try, attempt.

conquīrō, -ere, -quīsīvī, -quīsītum (v.t.): to search out, look for.

consanguineus, -i (adj. used as m. noun): kinsman, relative.

consciscō, -ere, -scīvī, -scitum (v.t.): to determine; consciscere sibi mortem: to kill oneself.

conscius, -a, -um: conscious of (with *dat.*, '. . . in one-self ').

conscrībō, ere, -scripsī, -scriptum (*v.t.*): to enlist, levy, raise.

consensus, -ūs (*m.*): agreement, consent.

consequor, -ī, -secūtus sum (*v.t.*): to overtake; to get, obtain.

consīdō, -ere, -sēdī, -sessum (*v.i.*): to take up position.

consilium, -ii (*n.*): plan, scheme; policy, strategy; council of war; resolution, purpose; **eo consilio ut . . .**: with the intention of . . .

consistō, -ere, -stitī, -stitum (*v.i.*): to stand, stand firm, take position, halt.

consōlor, -ārī, -ātus sum (*v.t.*): to console.

conspectus, -ūs (*m.*): sight, full view.

conspiciō, -ere, -spexī, -spectum (*v.t.*): to see, catch sight of.

conspicor, -ārī, -ātus sum (*v.t.*): to see, notice.

constantia, -ae (*f.*): resolution, determination, steadfastness.

constituō, -ere, -uī, -ūtum (*v.t.*): to settle, place, station, fix, decide.

consuescō, -ere, -ēvī, -ētum (*v.i.*): to become accustomed; (*in perfect*), to be accustomed.

consuetūdo, -inis (*f.*): custom, habit, experience, way.

consul, -is (*m.*): consul.

consulātus, -ūs (*m.*): consulate, office of consul.

consulō, -ere, -uī, sultum (*v.t.*): to consult.

consultum, -i (*n.*): decree, decision.

consūmo, -ere, -mpsī, -mptum (*v.t.*): consume, use up.

contendō, -ere, -dī, -tentum (*v.i.*): to strive, struggle, fight; to try hard, to hurry; to beg earnestly; to march, make for.

contentio, -ōnis (*f.*): dispute, rivalry.

continenter (*adv.*): continuously, without stopping.

contineō, -ēre, -uī, -tentum (*v.t.*): to bound, hold back, keep in, enclose.

contingō, -ere, -tigī, -tactum (*v.t. often v.i.*): to reach; to happen, fall to the lot of . . .

continuus, -a, -um: continuous, in succession.

contrā (*prep.* with *acc.*): against, in reply to.

contrahō, -ere, -xī, -ctum (*v.t.*): to bring together, concentrate.

contumēlia, -ae (*f.*): insult.

conveniō, -īre, -vēnī, -ventum (*v.i.*): to come together, agree; (*v.t.*): to meet.

conventus, -ūs (*m.*): conference; provincial assembly, assizes.

convertō, -ere, -tī, -versum (*v.t.*): to turn, change; **in fugam converto**: to put to flight, rout; **signa converto**: to face about.

convincō, -ere, -vīcī, -victum (*v.t.*): to prove.

convocō, -āre, -āvī, -ātum (*v.t.*): to summon, call together.

cōpia, -ae (*f.*): number, quantity, supply; plenty, wealth; **copiam faciō**: to supply; in *pl.*: forces.

cōpiōsus, -a, -um: rich, wealthy.

cōram (adv.): in one's own person; coram adsum: to be present in person, to be on the spot.

cornu, -ūs (n.): wing (of an army).

corpus, -oris (n.): body.

cotīdiānus, -a, -um: daily, usual.

cotīdiē (adv.): day by day, daily.

cremō, -āre, -āvī, -ātum (v.t.): to burn.

creō, -āre, -āvī, -ātum (v.t.): to appoint.

crescō, -ere, crēvī, crētum (v.i.): to become powerful, come to the front.

cruciātūs, -ūs (m.): torture.

crūdēlitās, -ātis (f.): cruelty.

crūdēliter (adv.): cruelly.

cultus, -ūs (m.): culture, civilisation, way of life.

cum (1) (prep. with abl.): with; (2) (conj.): when, before the time when (ch. xxiii); since; whereas, although; cum . . . tum: not only . . . but also; both . . . and.

cupidē, -ius, -issime (adv.): eagerly.

cupiditās, -ātis (f.): desire.

cupidus, -a, -um: eager; eager for, desirous of.

cupiō, -ere, -īvī, -ītum (v.t.): to wish, desire; (v.i. with dat.): to be well disposed towards, to favour.

cūr (adv.): why.

cūra, -ae (f.): care, attention, duty; ea res mihi curae erit: I will look after it.

cūrō, -āre, -āvī, -ātum (v.t.): to attend to, have a thing done.

cursus, -ūs (m.): running, speed.

custōs, -ōdis (m.): guard, spy.

damnō, -āre, -āvī, -ātum (v.t.): to condemn.

dē (prep. with abl.): down from, from, about, of, for; qua de causa: for which reason.

dēbeō, -ēre, -uī, -itum (v.t.): to owe, be obliged, be forced; I ought.

dēcēdō, -ere, -cessī, cessum (v.i.): to depart, leave, retire.

decem (num. adj.): ten.

dēcertō, -āre, -āvī, -atum (v.i.): to fight it out.

dēcidō, -ere, -dī (v.i.): to fall down from.

decimus, -a, -um: tenth.

dēcipiō, -ere, -cēpī, -ceptum (v.t.): to deceive, mislead.

dēclārō, -āre, -āvī, -atum (v.t.): to announce, declare.

decurio, -ōnis (m.): decurion, commander of troop of 10 cavalry.

dēditīcius, -ī (m.): one who has surrendered, prisoner.

dēditiō, -ōnis (f.): surrender, capitulation.

dēdō, -ere, -didī, -ditum (v.t.): to surrender, give up.

dēdūcō, ere, -dūxī, -ductum (v.t.): to lead away, withdraw.

dēfatigō, -āre, -āvī, -ātum (v.t.): to exhaust.

dēfendō, -ere, -dī, -sum (v.t.): to defend, protect; defendo bellum: to resist attack.

dēfessus, -a, -um: exhausted.

dēiciō, -ere, -iēcī, -iectum (v.t.): to cast down, disappoint.

deinde (*adv.*): then, next, secondly.

dēlīberō, -āre, -āvī, -ātum (*v.i.*): to consider, think over.

dēligō, -āre, -āvī, -ātum (*v.t.*): to bind, fasten, moor (a ship).

dēligō, -ere, -lēgī, -lectum (*v.t.*): to choose.

dēminuō, -ere, -uī, -ūtum (*v.t.*): to lessen, diminish.

dēmittō, -ere, -mīsī, -missum (*v.t.*): to let fall; **capite dēmisso**: with hanging heads.

dēmonstrō, -āre, -āvī, -ātum (*v.t.*): to show, point out.

dēmum (*adv.*): at last.

dēnegō, -āre, -āvī, -ātum (*v.t.*): to deny.

dēnī, -ae, -a (*distrib. num.*): ten each.

dēnique (*adv.*): finally.

dēnuntiō, -āre, -āvī, -ātum (*v.t.*): to threaten.

dēperdō, -ere, -didī, -ditum (*v.t.*): to lose.

dēpōnō, -ere, -suī, -situm (*v.t.*): to lay aside, put down.

dēpopulor, -ārī, -ātus sum (*v.t.*): to ravage; the *perf. part.* is used as a *passive*.

dēprecātor, -ōris (*m.*): pleader, advocate.

dēserō, -ere, -uī, -tum (*v.t.*): to forsake, desert.

dēsignō, -āre, -āvī, -ātum (*v.t.*): to indicate.

dēsistō, -ere, -stitī, -stitum (*v.i.*): to cease from, stop, abandon.

dēspērō, -āre, -āvī, -ātum (*v.i.*): to despair.

dēspiciō, -ere, -spexī, -spectum (*v.t.*): to despise.

dēstituō, -ere, -uī, -ūtum (*v.t.*): to abandon, desert, leave in the lurch.

dēstringō, -ere, -strinxī, -strictum (*v.t.*): to draw (a sword).

dēsum, -esse, -fuī (*v.i.*): to be lacking, to fail.

dēsuper (*adv.*): from above.

dēterior, -ius (*comp. adj.*): worse, smaller.

dēterreō, -ēre, -uī, -itum (*v.t.*): frighten from, deter, prevent.

dētrahō, -ere, -xī, -ctum (*v.t.*): to take away, remove.

dētrīmentum, -i (*n.*): loss, harm.

deus, -i (*m.*): god.

dexter, -tra, -trum (or **-tera, -terum**): right, on the right.

dextra, -ae (*f.*): right hand.

dīcio, -ōnis (*f.*): authority, rule.

dīcō, -ere, dixī, dictum (*v.t.*): to say, speak, tell; to name; **causam dīco**: to plead one's case, be tried.

dictio, ōnis (*f.*): pleading (see **dico**, above); **causae dictio**: trial.

dictum, -i (*n.*): word, command; **dicto audiens**: obedient.

diēs, -ēi (*m.* or *f.* in *sing.*, *m.* in *pl.*): day, date; **multo die**: late in the day.

differō, -ferre, distulī, dīlātum (*v.i.*): to differ.

difficilis, -e: hard, difficult.

dignitās, -ātis (*f.*): worth, dignity, honour, greatness.

dīligentia, -ae (*f.*): care, attention; careful planning.

dīmittō, -ere, -mīsī, -missum (*v.t.*): to send away, dismiss.

dīrimō, -ere, -ēmī, -emptum (v.t.): to break off, put to an end.

discēdō, -ere, -cessī, -cessum (v.i.): to go away, leave, forsake.

disciplīna, -ae (f.): training.

discō, -ere, didicī (v.t.): to learn.

disiciō, -ere, -iēcī, -iectum (v.t.): to scatter.

dispergō, -ere, -sī, -sum (v.t.): to scatter.

dispōnō, -ere, -posuī, -positum (v.t.): to dispose, station, post.

dītissimus: see dives.

diū, diūtius, diūtissimē (adv.): for a long time.

diurnus, -a, -um: by day.

diūturnitās, -ātis (f.): length (of time), long duration.

diūturnus, -a, -um: long, lasting a long time.

dīves, dītior, dītissimus: wealthy.

dīvidō, -ere, -vīsī, -vīsum (v.t.): to divide.

do, dare, dedī, datum (v.t.): to give; to cause.

doceō, -ēre, docuī, doctum (v.t.): to tell, point out.

doleō, -ēre, -uī, -itum (v.i.): to grieve, be sorry.

dolor, -ōris (m.): grief, pain, annoyance, chagrin; dolore adfici: to be chagrined.

dolus, -ī (m.): deceit, trickery.

domicilium, -ī (n.): home.

domus, -ūs (f.): house, home; domum: homewards, (to) home; domi: at home, among one's own people.

dōnō, -āre, -āvī, -ātum (v.t.): to present, give.

dubitātiō, -ōnis (f.): hesitation, doubt.

dubitō, -āre, -āvī, -ātum (v.i.): to doubt, hesitate.

dubium, -i (n. of dubius, -a, -um): doubt.

ducentī, -ae, -a: 200.

dūcō, -ere, duxī, ductum (v.t.): to lead, bring, draw; to marry (in matrimonium —of the husband) (cf. nubo): to prolong, to put off.

dum (conj.): while, until.

duo, duae, duo: two.

duodecim: 12.

dūrus, -a, -um: hard, difficult; si quid erat durius: if their comrades were hard pressed.

dux, ducis (m.): leader, commander, guide.

ē, ex (before vowels) (prep. with abl.): out of, from; of; by; on account of; after; ex usu: to the advantage of . . .; ex aliis: above all the others.

ēdō, ēdere, ēdidī, ēditum (v.t.): to show; . . . exempla cruciatusque: to employ every kind of torture.

ēdūcō, -ere, -xī, -ctum (v.t.): to lead out, bring out.

effēminō, -āre, -āvī, -ātum (v.t.): to make womanly, weaken.

efferō, -ferre, extulī, ēlātum (v.t.): to bring out; to make known, spread abroad.

efficiō, -ere, -fēcī, -fectum (v.t.): to make.

ēgredior, -ī, -gressus sum (v.i.): to leave.

ēgregius, -a, -um: outstanding.

ēlātum: see effero, above.

ēmigrō, -āre, -āvī, ātum
(v.i.): to emigrate.

ēmittō, -ere, -mīsī, -missum
(v.t.): to let go, drop.

emō, emere, ēmī, emptum
(v.t.): to buy.

enim (conj., 2nd word in
clause): for.

ēnuntiō, -āre, -āvī, -ātum
(v.t.): to make known, disclose.

eō, īre, īvī or iī, itum (v.i.):
to go.

eō (adv.): thither, there; eo ...
imponere: to mount ... on
them (the horses) (thereon).

eō (abl. of id) (in several
phrases): by so much; eo ...
quo: the more ... the more;
eo magis: all the more;
eo ... quod: for the reason
that ..., because.

eōdem (adv.): to the same
place, in the same direction;
to the same conclusion.

eques, -itis (m.): horseman;
in pl., cavalry.

equester, -tre: of the cavalry,
cavalry.

equitātus, -tūs (m.): cavalry,
knights, nobles.

equus, -ī (m.): horse; ad
equum rescribo: to enrol
among the knights, to make
one a knight.

ēripiō, -ere, -ripuī, -reptum
(v.t.): to snatch away from,
take away; to rescue, save.

et (conj.): and, also; et ... et:
both ... and.

etiam (conj.): also, even.

etsī (conj.): although.

ēvellō, -ere (perfect, rare;
-ī or -vulsī), -vulsum (v.t.):
to tear out.

excipiō, -ere, -cēpī, -ceptum
(v.t.): to receive.

exemplum, -ī (n.): example,
precedent (see edo, above).

exeō, -īre, -iī, -itum (v.i.):
to go out, leave.

exerceō, -ēre, uī, -itum
(v.t.): to train.

exercitātio, -onis (f.): training.

exercitātus, -a, -um (perf.
part. pass. of exercitō, -āre):
trained, experienced.

exercitus, -ūs (m.): army.

existimātio, -ōnis (f.):
opinion, reputation.

existimō, -āre, -āvī, -ātum
(v.t.): to think.

expedītus, -a, -um (perf. part.
pass. of expediō, -īre):
open, free, unencumbered,
mobile; in light marching
order, without baggage, in
battle order.

experior, īrī, -pertus sum
(v.t.): to try, experience.

explōrātor, -ōris (m.): scout,
spy; (pl.), reconnaissance
force.

exprimō, -ere, -pressī, -pres-
sum (v.t.): to press out,
extract.

expugnō, -āre, -āvī, -ātum
(v.t.): to capture, storm (a
town, camp, etc.).

exquīrō, -ere, -quīsīvī, -quī-
sītum (v.t.): to inquire
closely, ascertain.

exsequor, -ī, -secūtus sum
(v.t.): to carry out, assert.

exspectō, -āre, -āvī, -ātum
(v.t.): to await, expect; also
v.i.: to wait.

extrā (prep. with acc.): outside, beyond.

extrēmus, -a, -um: furthest,
last; extremum (n.): end,
extremity.

exūrō, -ere, -ussī, ustum (*v.t.*): to burn.

facile, -ius, -illimē (*adv.*): easily.

facilis, -e: easy.

facinus, -oris (*n.*): deed, offence, fault.

faciō, -ere, fēcī, factum (*v.t.*): to make, construct, do, act, behave; **vim facio**: to use force; **iter facio**: to march, travel; **copiam facio**: to provide; **periculum facio**: to try, test; **sui potestatem facere**: to let (them) get near him; **proelium facio**: to fight. See also **fīo**, below.

factio, -ōnis (*f.*): party.

factum, -ī (*n.*): deed, action.

facultās, -ātis (*f.*): ability, power, permission, advantage, opportunity; supply; in *pl.*: (not,) resources.

famēs, -is (*f.*): hunger.

familia, -ae (*f.*): household, retinue.

familiāris, -e: personal; **res familiaris**: personal property; (used as *noun. m.*): close friend.

fās, (*indecl. n.*): the will of the gods; as *adj*: right, allowed.

fātum, -ī (*n.*): destiny, fate.

faveō, -ēre, fāvī, fautum (*v.i.*): to favour, support.

fēlīcitās, -ātis (*f.*): happiness, prosperity, success.

ferē (*adv.*): almost, nearly; mostly.

ferō, ferre, tulī, lātum (*v.t.*): to bear, carry, bring; to regard; to endure, put up with; **graviter fero**: to be angry at; **signa fero**: to march, advance.

ferrum, -ī (*n.*): iron, point; weapon, sword.

ferus, -a, -um: fierce.

fidēs, -ēī (*f.*): loyalty, confidence; promise; trust.

fīlia, -ae (*f.*): daughter.

fīlius, -ii (*m.*): son.

fingō, -ere, finxī, fictum (*v.t.*): to feign, pretend: **voltum fingo**: to pretend to be cheerful.

fīnis, -is (*m.*): end; (in *pl.*): frontier, territory, country.

fīnitimus, -a, -um: neighbouring; (as *noun. m.*): neighbour.

fīo, fierī, factus sum (*v.i.*: used as *pass.* of facio): to be made, to be done, to happen; **his rebus fiebat ut**: the result (of this) was that.

firmus, -a, -um: strong, stable, sound, sure.

flāgitō, -āre, -āvī, -ātum (*v.t.*): to demand, ask again and again.

fleō, flēre, flēvī, flētum (*v.i.*): to weep.

flētus, -ūs (*m.*): weeping.

flōrens, -ntis (*pr. part.* of flōreō): prosperous, flourishing; **florentissimis rebus**: though they were at the height of their power and prosperity.

flūmen, -inis (*n.*): river, stream.

fluō, -ere, fluxī, fluxum (*v.i.*): to flow.

fore (*fut. inf.* of sum); **fore utī**: it would so happen that.

fortis, -e: brave.

fortitūdo, -inis (*f.*): bravery.

fortūna, -ae (*f.*): fortune, chance, luck, plight; (in *pl.*): possessions.

fossa, -ae (*f.*): ditch, trench.
frangō, -ere, frēgī, fractum (*v.t.*): to break, destroy.
frāter, -tris (*m.*): brother.
frāternus, -a, -um: brotherly; **fraternum nomen**: title of 'brothers' . . .
frīgus, -oris (*n.*): cold.
fructuōsus, -a, -um: fruitful, fertile, rich.
frūges, -um (*pl.* of *defective noun* **frux,** *f.*): crops.
frūmentarius, -a, -um: productive; **res frumentaria**: supplies, commissariat.
frūmentum, -ī (*n.*): corn, grain, provisions; (in *pl.*): crops.
fuga, -ae (*f.*): flight, escape.
fugiō, -ere, fūgī, fugītum (*v.i.*): to fly, run away.
fugitīvus, -ī (*m.*): fugitive, deserter; runaway slave.
furor, -ōris (*m.*): madness, fury.

Gallicus, -a, -um: Gallic, of Gaul (used of *things*).
Gallus, -a, -um: Gallic (used of *people*).
generātim (*adv.*): by tribes, in separate tribes.
genus, -eris (*n.*): sort, kind; race, family.
gerō, -ere, gessī, gestum (*v.t.*): to carry on, carry out, do, accomplish; (in *pass.*): to happen, go on; **bellum gero**: to make war.
gladius, -iī (*m.*): sword.
glōria, -ae (*f.*): glory, reputation.
glōrior, -ārī, -ātus sum (*v.i.*): to boast.
Graecus, -a, -um: Greek.

grandis, -e: big, great.
grātia, -ae (*f.*): favour, popularity, esteem, influence; gratitude, debt of gratitude; (in *pl.*): thanks; **gratias ago**: to thank.
grātūlātio, -ōnis (*f.*): congratulation, occasion for congratulation; thanksgiving, rejoicing.
grātulor, -ārī, -ātus sum (*v.i.*): to congratulate.
grātulor, -ārī, -ātus sum (*v.i.*): to congratulate.
grātus, -a, -um: welcome, agreeable, pleasant; **gratum, -ī** (*n.* of *adj.*): a favour.
gravis, -e: heavy, serious, severe.
graviter, -ius, -issimē (*adv.*): seriously, heavily; **graviter fero**: to be angry at; **graviter statuo in**: to deal severely with.
gravor, -ārī, -ātus sum (*v.i.*): to be angry, complain.

habeō, -ēre, -uī, -itum (*v.t.*): to have, hold, possess; to reckon, think; **habeo in loco . . .**: to reckon as, treat as; **habeo pro**: to regard as; **habeo orationem**: to make a speech.
hīberna, -ōrum (*n. pl.*): winter quarters.
hīc, haec, hōc (*dem. adj.*): this; (used as *pron.*): he, she, it, they.
hīc (*adv.*): here.
hiemō, -āre, -āvī, -ātum (*v.i.*): to winter, spend the winter.
hōc (*abl. n. sing.* of **hīc**): because of this.

homo, -inis (*m.* sometimes *f.*): human being, man; (in *pl.*): people, population.

honestus, -a, -um: noble, distinguished.

honor, -ōris (*m.*): honour, esteem, distinction.

honōrificus, -a, -um: honourable.

hōra, -ae (*f.*): hour.

horreō, -ēre, -uī (*v.i.* also *v.t.*): to shudder; to shudder at, be terrified of.

hortor, -ārī, -ātus sum (*v.t.*): to urge, encourage.

hospes, -itis (*m.*): guest, host, friend.

hospitium, -iī (*n.*): hospitality, friendship.

hostis, -is (*m.*): enemy; (often in *pl.*).

hūc (*adv.*): hither, to this place; (we often say in English ' here ').

hūmānitās, -ātis (*f.*): culture, civilisation, civilised way of life.

iactō, -āre, -āvī, -atum (*v.t.*): to toss, shake; to discuss, talk about.

iam (*adv.*): now, by now; already; then, by then; **non iam**: no longer.

ibi (*adv.*): there, in that place.

ictus, -ūs (*m.*): blow.

īdem, eadem, idem (*pron.* or *adj.*): the same.

idōneus, -a, -um: suitable, convenient.

Idūs, -uum (*f. pl.*): the Ides (13th or 15th of month: often abbreviated to Id.).

ignis, -is (*m.*): fire; **ignī cremō** or **necō**: to burn to death.

ignōrō, -āre, -āvī, -ātum (*v.t.*): not to know; to overlook.

ignoscō, -ere, -nōvī, -nōtum (*v.t.*): to pardon, forgive.

illātus: from **inferō** (see below).

ille, -a, -ud (*dem. adj.*): that; (used as *pron.*): he, she, it, they.

illīc (*adv.*): there.

immortālis, -e: immortal.

impedīmentum, -i (*n.*): hindrance, handicap; (in *pl.*): baggage, equipment.

impediō, -īre, -īvī, -ītum (*v.t.*): to hamper, hinder, impede, encumber.

impellō, -ere, -pulī, -pulsum (*v.t.*): to push forward, drive.

impendeō, -ēre (no *perf.* or *sup.*, *v.i.*): to overhang.

imperātor, -ōris (*m.*): general, commander-in-chief.

imperītus, -a, -um: inexperienced.

imperium, -iī (*n.*): authority, command, government, power; (in *pl.*) tyranny.

imperō, -āre, -āvī, -ātum (*v.a.*): to command, order; to demand; to tyrannise (with *dat.* of person commanded, *acc.* of thing demanded or ordered).

impetrō, -āre, -āvī, -ātum (*v.a.*): to get a request granted; to obtain.

impetus, -ūs (*m.*): attack, charge; **impetum faciō**: to charge.

implōrō, -āre, -āvī, -ātum (*v.t.*): to implore, beg for.

impōnō, -ere, posuī, -positum (*v.t.*): to put in, to put on, impose; to mount (on a horse).

importō, -āre, -āvī, -ātum
(*v.t.*): to bring in, import,
introduce.

improbus, -a, -um: wicked,
bad, impudent.

imprōvīsō (*adv.*): unexpected-
ly.

impugnō, -āre, -āvī, -ātum
(*v.t.*): to attack.

impūne (*adv.*): with impunity,
safely.

impūnitās, -ātis (*f.*): impunity, freedom from punishment.

in (*prep.* with *acc.*): into, to,
towards, on, against, at;
into the hands (of): (of
time) for; (with *abl.*): in, on,
among, over; considering
the . . .; **in armis**: under
arms, at readiness; **in primis**: first, at first.

incendō, -ere, -dī, -sum
(*v.t.*): to burn.

incidō, -ere, -dī, -cāsum
(*v.i.*): to fall in with, fall
into the hands of, meet by
chance.

incitō, -āre, -āvī, -ātum
(*v.t.*): to excite, encourage,
arouse, enrage.

incolō, -ere, -coluī, -cultum
(*v.t.* sometimes *v.i.*): to
inhabit, live in; to dwell.

incolumis, -e: safe, unharmed.

incommodum, -ī (*n.* of *adj.*):
misfortune, disaster.

incrēdibilis, -e: incredible.

incūsō, -āre, -āvī, ātum
(*v.t.*): to blame, rebuke.

inde (*adv.*): from there, thence.

indicium, -iī (*n.*): information; **per indicium**: by
informers.

indīcō, -ere, -dixī, -dictum
(*v.t.*): to proclaim, call.

indūcō, -ere, -duxī, -ductum
(*v.t.*): to induce, lead on,
persuade, influence.

indulgeō, -ēre, -sī, -tum
(*v.t.*): to favour, be kind to.

inermus, -a, -um: unarmed.

inferior, -ius (*comp. adj.* from
infrā): lower.

inferō, -ferre, -tulī, illatum
(*v.t.*): to bring in; to inflict,
give; **bellum infero**: to
make war on, invade; **causam infero**: to put forward,
plead, a reason; **signa
infero**: to advance.

inflectō, -ere, -flexī, flexum
(*v.t.*): to bend.

influō, -ere, -fluxī, -fluxum
(*v.i.*): to flow into.

ingens, -entis: huge.

iniciō, -ere, -iēcī, iectum
(*v.t.*): to put in, arouse in.

inimīcus, -a, -um: unfriendly,
hostile; (as *noun.*, *m.*): enemy,
opponent.

inīquus, -a, -um: unjust,
unfair, in the wrong.

initium, -iī (*n.*): beginning;
initium capio: to begin.

iniūria, -ae (*f.*): injury,
wrong; in *abl.*: wrongfully.

iniussū (*abl. m.*, not found in
other cases): without orders
(**suo**: from him).

innascor, -ī, -nātus sum
(*v.i.*): to be produced, to
arise.

innocentia, -ae (*f.*): blame-
lessness, uprightness.

inopia, -ae (*f.*): shortage,
want.

inopinans, -ntis (*adj.*): not
expecting, unawares, off one's
guard.

insciens, -ntis (*adj.*): not
knowing, ignorant.

insequor, -ī, -secūtus sum (*v.t.*): to follow, follow up, pursue.

insidiae, -ārum (*f.* only in *pl.*): ambush; trickery, treachery.

insigne, -is (*n.*): badge, sign; (often in *pl.*, **insignia**): uniform.

insignis, -e: notable, outstanding.

insiliō, -īre, -uī (*v.i.*): to leap on.

insolenter (*adv.*): insolently, haughtily.

instituō, -ere, -uī, -ūtum (*v.t.*): to train, bring up.

institūtum, -ī (*n.*): custom, determination.

instō, -āre, -itī (*v.i.*): to press forward, drive on; to be near.

instruō, -ere, -uxī, -uctum (*v.t.*): to draw up, dispose.

intellegō (or **-igō**), **-ere, -lexī, -lectum** (*v.t.*): to know, understand; to get to know, find out, realise, see.

inter (*prep.* with *acc.*): among, between; during, in the course of; **inter se**: each other.

intercēdō, -ere, -cessī, -cessum (*v.i.*): to come between, lie between, exist between; to elapse, pass.

interclūdō, -ere, -ūsī, -ūsum (*v.t.*): to cut off, shut off.

interdīcō, -ere, -dixī, -dictum (*v.t.*): to forbid (*dat.* of person; *abl.* of thing or place).

interdiū (*adv.*): by day.

interdum (*adv.*): sometimes.

intereā (*adv.*): meanwhile.

interficiō, -ere, -fēcī, -fectum (*v.t.*): to kill.

interim (*adv.*): meanwhile.

intermittō, -ere, -mīsī, -missum (*v.t.*): to put between, interpose; to interrupt, discontinue; (in *pass.*, almost like a *dep. vb.*) to pass; (as *v.i.*) to leave a gap.

internecio, -ōnis (*f.*): massacre.

interpellō, -āre, -āvī, -ātum (*v.t.*): to interrupt, molest, obstruct.

interpōnō, -ere, -posuī, -positum (*v.t.*): to bring forward, interpose.

interpres, -etis (*m.*): interpreter.

intersum, -esse, fuī (*v.i.*): to be between.

intervallum, -ī (*n.*): interval, distance.

intrā (*prep.* with *acc.*): within.

intueor, -ērī, -uitus sum (*v.t.*): to gaze upon.

inveniō, -īre, -vēnī, -ventum (*v.t.*): to find.

invictus, -a, -um: unconquered, invincible.

invītō, -āre, -āvī, -ātum (*v.t.*): to invite.

invītus, -a, -um: unwilling; **se invito**: against his will.

ipse, -a, -um (*pron.* or *adj.*): -self, -selves.

īrācundus, -a, -um: hot-tempered, angry.

irrīdiculē (*adv.*): unwittily; **non irrīdicule**: wittily.

is, ea, id (*dem. adj.* or *pron.*): that, this; he, she, it, they; such.

ita (*adv.*): thus, so, in such a way.

itaque (*conj.*): so, therefore, and so.

item (*adv.*, sometimes as *conj.*): also, likewise, moreover.

iter, itineris (*n.*): road, route, way, journey, march; stage (of journey), a day's journey or march; line of march; **magnum iter:** a forced march; **iter facio:** to march, travel.

iterum (*adv.*): again, a second time.

iuba, -ae (*f.*): mane.

iubeō, -ēre, inssī, iussum (*v.t.*): to command, order.

iūdicium, -iī (*n.*): judgment, decision, opinion; trial; **optimum iudicium facio de . . .:** to think very highly of.

iūdicō, -āre, -āvī, -ātum (*v.t.*): to judge, consider, conclude that, determine.

iugum, -ī (*n.*): yoke, hill.

iūmentum, -ī (*n.*): baggage-animal, beast of burden.

iungō, -ere, -nxī, -nctum (*v.t.*): to join, fasten together.

iūrō, -āre, āvī, -ātum (*v.i.*): to swear, take an oath.

iūs, iuris (*n.*): right, law; rights; authority, sphere of authority.

iūs iūrandum, iūris iūrandī (*n.*, also written as one word): oath.

iustitia, -ae (*f.*): justice.

iustus, -a, -um: just, proper, due.

iuvō, -āre, iūvī, iūtum (*v.t.*): to help, aid.

Kal.: Kalendae, -arum (*f.*): the Kalends, the first day of the month.

L.: Lucius (Roman *praenomen*).

labor, -ōris (*m.*): toil, trouble.

labōrō, -āre, -āvī, -ātum (*v.i.*): to be in difficulties; to be anxious.

lacessō, -ere, -īvī, -ītum (*v.t.*): to harass, harry, attack.

lacrima, -ae (*f.*): tear.

lacus, -ūs (*m.*): lake.

lapis, -idis (*m.*): stone.

largior, -īrī, -ītus sum (*v.i.*): to give lavish presents, to bribe.

largiter (*adv.*): widely; **largiter posse:** to have very widespread power.

largītio, -ōnis (*f.*): generosity; bribe.

latē (*adv.*): widely.

lātitūdo, -inis (*f.*): breadth, width.

lātus, -a, -um: wide, broad.

latus, -eris (*n.*): side, flank.

laus, -dis (*f.*): praise, credit, glory.

lēgātio, -onis (*f.*): embassy, mission.

lēgātus, -i (*m.*): (a person to whom a duty is delegated); envoy, deputy-commander, ambassador, representative.

legio, -ōnis (*f.*): legion.

legiōnārius, -a, -um: belonging to a legion; **legionarius miles:** a legionary (soldier); (also used as *noun*).

lēnitās, -ātis (*f.*): gentleness, slowness.

lex, lēgis (*f.*): law.

libenter (*adv.*): willingly.

līber, -era, -erum: free, unchecked.

līberalitās, -ātis (*f.*): generosity.

liberē, -ius, -errimē: freely.

liberi, -orum (*m.*): children.

libertās, -ātis (*f.*): liberty, freedom.

liceor, -ērī, -itus sum (*v.i.*): to bid.

licet, -uit (or **licitum est**) (*impersonal v.*): it is allowed; **id per se fieri licere:** (he allowed it to happen), he agreed.

lingua, -ae (*f.*): tongue, language.

linter, -tris (*f.*): boat.

littera, -ae (*f.*): a letter (of the alphabet), character; (in *pl.*), a letter (correspondence), despatch.

locus, -ī (*m.*) (in *pl.*, **loca, -ōrum,** *n.*): place, space, ground; locality, district; **locī natura:** natural barriers; **eodem loco habeo:** to regard . . . in the same way as . . .

longē, -ius, -issimē (*adv.*): far, further, furthest; by far.

longinquus, -a, -um: long, long lasting, distant.

longitūdo, -inis (*f.*): length.

longus, -a, -um: long, distant.

loquor, -ī, locūtus sum (*v.t.*): to speak, say, talk.

lūna, -ae (*f.*): moon.

lux, lūcis (*f.*): light, daylight; **prima luce:** at dawn.

M (for **mille**): 1,000.

M.: Marcus (Roman *praenomen*).

magis (*comp.* of **magnopere,** *adv.*): more; **eo magis:** so much the more . . .

magistrātus, -ūs (*m.*): magistrate, official, chieftain; magistracy, chieftainship.

magnitūdo, -inis (*f.*): greatness, size.

magnō opere (also **magnopere**) (*adv.*): greatly, very; **magnopere tribuo:** to give *too* much credit to.

magnus, -a, -um: large, big, great; **magnum iter:** a forced march.

māior, -us (*comp.* of **magnus**): greater; (*pl.* **māiorēs**): forefathers, ancestors.

male (*adv.*): badly, unsuccessfully.

maleficium, -ii (*n.*): harm, damage.

malus, -a, -um: bad; **malum, -ī** (as *n.*): evil.

mandātum, -i (*n.* of *perf. pass. part.* of **mando**): instruction, message; (in *pl.*): message.

mandō, -āre, -āvī, -ātum (*v.t.*): to entrust, give a task; **se fugae mandare:** to take to flight.

maneō, -ēre, -sī, -sum (*v.i.*): to stay, remain; **maneo in:** abide by, hold to.

manus, -ūs (*f.*): hand; band, party, force.

matara, -ae (*f.*): pike (weapon)

māter, -tris (*f.*): mother; **matres familiae:** the matrons, married women.

mātrimōnium, -ii (*n.*): marriage; **in matrimonium duco:** to marry.

mātūrē, -ius, -urrimē (*adv.*): early.

mātūrō, -āre, -āvī, -ātum (*v.i.*): to hurry, hasten.

mātūrus, -a, -um: early, ripe.

maximē (*sup. adv.*): most, outstandingly, especially, very, chiefly.

maximus, -a, -um (*sup.* of **magnus**): greatest, biggest, very great; principal.

mediocriter (*adv.*): moderately; **non mediocriter**: very greatly.

medius, -a, -um: middle, in the middle of; half-way up; half-way between.

memoria, -ae (*f.*): memory; **memoriā teneo**: to remember; **memoriā patrum**: in the time of our fathers.

mens, mentis (*f.*): mind.

mensis, -is (*m.*): month.

mercātor, -ōris (*m.*): trader, merchant.

mercēs, -ēdis (*f.*): pay.

mereō, -ēre, -uī, -itum (*v.t.*, also **mereor, -ērī, -itus sum**): to earn, deserve, gain.

merīdiēs, -ēī (*f.*): midday; south.

meritum, -i (*n.*): deserts, merits; service; **merito accidere**: be deserved by.

mētior, -īrī, mensus sum (*v.t.*): to distribute, issue. This *dep. verb.* is *passive* in ch. xli.

mīles, -itis (*m.*): soldier.

mīlia, -ium (*n. noun.*): thousands.

mīlitāris, -e: military; **rei militaris peritissimus**: a most experienced soldier.

mille (*indecl. num. adj.*):1,000; **mille passūs**: a mile; also **mille** (*noun*) **passuum. C mīlia passuum**: 100 miles (see **mīlia**, above).

minimē (*sup. adv.*): least, very little, not at all.

minimum (*adv.*): very little; **minimum possum**: to have very little power.

minimus, -a, -um (*sup.* of **parvus**): least, smallest.

minor, -us (*comp.* of **parvus**): less, smaller.

minuō, -ere, -uī, -ūtum (*v.t.*): to diminish, lessen;

minus (*comp. adv.*): less, the less; (often almost=not); **non minus**: just as much.

mīror, -ārī, -ātūs sum (*v.t.*): to wonder, be surprised at.

mīrus, -a, -um: wonderful, surprising; **mirum in modum**: wonderfully.

miser, -a, -um: wretched, woeful.

miseror, -ārī, -ātus sum (*v.t.*): to lament, weep for.

mittō, -ere, mīsī, missum (*v.t.*): to send, throw.

modo (*adv.*): only, just.

modus, -ī (*m.*): measure, limit; way, fashion.

mōlimentum, -ī (*n.*): great effort.

mōlō, -ere, -uī, -itum (*v.t.*): to grind.

moneō, -ēre, -uī, -itum (*v.t.*): to warn, advise.

mons, -ntis (*m.*): mountain, hill.

morior, morī, mortuus sum (*v.i.*): to die.

moror, -ārī, -ātus sum (*v.t.*, sometimes *v.i.*): to delay, hold back, wait.

mors, -rtis (*f.*): death.

mortuus, -a, -um (*perf. part.* of **morior**, see above): dead.

mōs, mōris (*m.*): custom.

moveō, -ēre, mōvī, mōtum (*v.t.*): to move.

mulier, -is (*f.*): woman.

multī, -ae, -a: many.

multitūdo, -inis (*f.*): number, large number; crowd, people; **multitudo hominum**: size of population.

multō (*abl.* of **multum,** used as *adv.*): much (followed by comparatives).

multum (*adv.*): much, very.

multus, -a, -um: much; **multo die:** late in the day; **ad multam noctem:** far into the night.

mūniō, -īre, -īvī, -ītum (*v.t.*): to fortify, protect.

mūnitiō, -ōnis (*f.*): fortification, construction-work.

mūnus, -eris (*n.*): duty, gift.

mūrus, -ī (*m.*): wall.

nam, namque (*conj.*): for.

nanciscor, -ī, nactus sum (*v.t.*): to get, come upon.

nātiō, -ōnis (*f.*): nation, tribe.

nātūra, -ae (*f.*): nature, character.

nāvicula, -ae (*f.*): small boat.

nāvis, -is (*f.*): ship, boat.

nē: (1) (*adv.*): not (wishes and commands). (2) (*conj.*): so as not to, so that . . . not, not to (purpose); lest, that (after *verbs* of fearing).

nē . . . quidem (*adv.*): not even.

-ne: attached to first word of a question.

nec: see **neque.**

necessāriō (*adv.*): necessarily.

necessārius, -a, -um: necessary, urgent; (as *noun. m.*): close friend, kinsman.

necessitūdo, -inis (*f.*): friendship.

necne (*adv.*): or not.

necō, -āre, -āvī, -ātum (*v.t.*): to put to death; **igni neco:** to burn to death.

neglegō, -ere, -exī, -ectum (*v.t.*): to overlook.

negō, -āre, -āvī, -ātum (*v.t.*): to deny, to say that . . . not.

negōtium, -iī (*n.*): business, undertaking, task.

nēmō (*irreg.*): nobody, no one.

neque or **nec** (*conj.*): nor, and not; **neque . . . neque:** neither . . . nor.

nervus, -i (*m.*): sinew; (*pl.*) strength.

neu or **nēve** (*conj.*) (=**et ne**): and not to, etc.

nex, necis (*f.*): violent death, execution; **vitae necisque:** life and death.

nihil (*indecl. n.*): nothing; (used as *adv.*): not at all, not.

nihilō (*abl.* of **nihilum**): by nothing; **nihilo minus, nihilo sētius:** none the less, nevertheless.

nisi (*conj.*): if not, unless; without (being, etc.); except.

nitor, -ī, nīsus (nixus) sum (*v.i.*): to rely on.

nōbilis, -e: noble, distinguished; (as *n.*): a noble.

nōbilitās, -ātis (*f.*): nobility, the nobles.

noctū (*adv.*): by night.

nocturnus, -a, -um: nightly, in the night, night-.

nōlō, nolle, nōlui (*v.i.*): to be unwilling, to refuse.

nōmen, -inis (*n.*): name, title; **nomen capio:** become famous; **suo nomine:** on his own account.

nōminātim (*adv.*): by name.

nōn (*adv.*): not.

nōn nullī (*adj.,* or as *pron.*): some, a considerable number.

nōn nunquam (*adv.*): sometimes, repeatedly.

nōnāgintā (*num. adj.*): ninety.

nōndum (*adv.*): not yet.

Nōricus, -a, -um: of Noricum.

nōs: we.

noster, -tra, -trum: our; **nostrī**: our men, *i.e.* the Romans.

novem (*num. adj.*): nine.

novus, -a, -um: new, fresh; **novissimum agmen, novissimi**: the rearguard, the rear (of the column).

nox, noctis (*f.*): night; **ad multam noctem**: till far into the night; **prima nocte**: at nightfall.

nūbō, -ere, -psī, -ptum (*v.i.*): to marry (with *dat.*, only of the woman) (*cf.* **duco**); **nuptum colloco**: to give in marriage.

nūdus, -a, -um: uncovered, unprotected.

nullus, -a, -um: no, none.

num: introduces questions (*esp.* rhetorical) expecting *no* for answer; **num posse se**: could he . . .

numerus, -ī (*m.*): number, quantity.

numquam, nunquam (*adv.*): never.

nunc (*adv.*): now.

nuntiō, -āre, -āvī, -ātum (*v.t.*): to announce, tell, report, bring news of.

nuntius, -iī (*m.*): messenger, message.

nūper (*adv.*): recently, lately.

nūtus, -ūs (*m.*): nod, will.

ob (*prep.* with *acc.*): because of, on account of.

obaerātus, -i (*m.*): debtor.

obiciō, -ere, -iēcī, -iectum (*v.t.*): to expose, throw in the way.

oblīviscor, -ī, oblītus sum (with *gen.*): to forget.

obsecrō, -āre, -āvī, -ātum (*v.t.*): to beg, beseech, implore.

observō, -āre, -āvī, -ātum (*v.t.*): to observe.

obses, -sidis (*m.*, can be *f.*): hostage.

obsignō, -āre, -āvī, -atum (*v.t.*): to seal.

obstringō, -ere, -nxī, -strictum (*v.t.*): to bind, put under an obligation.

obtineō, -ēre, -uī, -tentum (*v.t.*): to hold; to get.

occāsus, ūs (*m.*): setting (of the sun); **occāsus sōlis**: sunset; the West.

occīdō, -ere, -dī, -sum (*v.t.*): to cut down, kill.

occultō, -āre, -āvī, -ātum (*v.t.*): to hide.

occultus, -a, -um: hidden, secret; **occultum, -ī, n.**: secrecy.

occupō, -āre, -āvī, -ātum (*v.t.*): to seize, occupy.

occurrō, -ere, -currī, -cursum (*v.i.*): to meet, stop, hinder.

ōceanus, -ī (*m.*): the Atlantic.

octo (*num.*): eight.

octōdecim (*num.*): eighteen.

octōgintā (*num.*): eighty.

oculus, -ī (*m.*): eye, sight.

ōdī, -isse (*v.t.*; *perf.* with *pres.* meaning): to hate.

offendō, -ere, -dī, -sum (*v.t.*): to offend, hurt.

offensio, -ōnis (*f.*): offence.

officium, -iī (*n.*): duty, loyalty; sense of duty; service; ability to do one's duty.

omnīno (*adv.*): altogether, in all, entirely; only; with *negs.*, at all.

omnis, -e: all, every; as a whole.

opēs, -um (*f. pl.*): resources, wealth; in *sing.*, **opem, opis**, defective: aid, strength.

oportet, -ēre, -uit (*imp. vb.*): it is right, it is necessary; **oportet me**: I have to . . . .

oppidum, -ī (*n.*): town.

opportūnus, -a, -um: suitable.

opprimō, -ere, -pressī, -pressum (*v.t.*): to crush, over-power.

oppugnō, -āre, -āvī, -ātum (*v.t.*): to attack.

optimē (*adv.*): very well.

optimus, -a, -um (*sup.* of **bonus**): very good, best.

opus, -eris (*n.*): work; military work, fortifications; **opus est**: is necessary, is needed; there is need of.

ōrātio, -ōnis (*f.*): speech; **orationem habeo**: to make a speech.

ordo, -inis (*m.*): rank, company (of soldiers).

oriens, -ntis (*pr. part.* of **orior**): **oriens sol**: the East.

orior, -īrī, ortus sum (*v.i.*): to arise, begin, start.

ornāmentum, -ī (*n.*): distinction.

ōrō, -āre, -āvī, -ātum (*v.t.*): to beg, pray, beseech.

ostendō, -ere, -dī, -tum (*v.t.*): to point out, show.

P.: Publius (Roman *praenomen*).

pābulātio, -ōnis (*f.*): foraging.

pābulum, -ī (*n.*): fodder.

pācō, -āre, -āvī, -ātum (*v.t.*): to subdue, pacify.

paene (*adv.*): nearly, almost.

pāgus, -ī (*m.*): canton, division of tribe.

palūs, -ūdis (*f.*): marsh.

pandō, -ere, -ī, -passum (also **pansum**) (*v.t.*): to stretch out.

pār, paris: equal, equal to, a match for.

parātus, -a, -um (*perf. part. pass.* of **parō, -āre**): ready.

pāreō, -ēre, -uī -itum (*v.i.*, used as *v.tr.*, with *dat.*): to obey.

parō, -āre, -āvī, -atum (*v.t.*): to prepare, get ready, get.

pars, -rtis (*f.*): part, side, direction; **qua ex parte**: on which account; **magna ex parte**: to a great extent; **tres partes**: three quarters.

parvus, -a, -um: small, low (price).

passus, -ūs (*m.*): pace; **mille passus**: a mile.

passus, -a, -um (*perf. pass. part.* of **pando**): outstretched.

patens, -ntis (*adj.*): open.

pateō, -ēre, -uī (*v.i.*): to extend, stretch, lie open.

pater, -tris (*m.*): father.

patior, -ī, passus sum (*v.t.*): to suffer, allow.

paucī, -ae, -a: few, a few.

paulātim (*adv.*): gradually, little by little.

paulō (*abl.*, used as *adv.* with *comps.*): (a) little.

paulum, -ī (*n.*): a little.

pax, pācis (*f.*): peace.

peccō, -āre, -āvī, -ātum (*v.i.*): to do wrong.

pedes, -itis (*m.*): foot-soldier; (in *pl.*): infantry.

pēior, -us (*comp.* of **malus**): worse.

pellō, -ere, pepulī, pulsum (*v.t.*): to drive back, drive, beat, repel.

pendō, -ere, pependī, pensum (*v.t.*): to pay.

per (*prep.* with *acc.*): through, by means of, by; **per se**: so far as he was concerned.

percontātio, -ōnis (*f.*): questioning, inquiry.

perdūcō, -ere, -duxī, -ductum (*v.t.*): to draw, construct.

pereō, -īre, -iī, -itum (*v.i.*): to perish.

perfacilis, -e: very easy.

perferō, -ferre, -tulī, -lātum (*v.t.*): to carry through, endure.

perficiō, -ere, -fēcī, -fectum (*v.t.*): to complete, accomplish, finish; to arrange, settle.

perfringō, -ere, -frēgī, -fractum (*v.t.*): to break through.

perfuga, -ae (*m.*): deserter.

perfugiō, -ere, -fūgī, -fugītum (*v.i.*): to desert.

perīculōsus, -a, -um: dangerous.

periculum, -ī (*n.*): danger, trial; **periculum faciō**: to try, try the mettle of.

peritus, -a, -um: experienced in.

permaneō, -ere, -mansī, -mansum (*v.t.*): to remain, stay.

permittō, -ere, -mīsī, -missum (*v.t.*): to allow, grant.

permoveō, -ēre, -mōvī, -mōtum (*v.t.*): to move deeply, sway, influence.

perniciēs, -ēī (*f.*): destruction.

perpaucī, -ae, -a: very few.

perpetuō (*adv.*): for ever.

perpetuus, -a, -um: perpetual, unbroken; **perpetua vita**: through his whole life.

perrumpō, -ere, -rūpī, -ruptum (*v.t.*): to break through.

persequor, -ī, -secūtus sum (*v.t.*): to pursue, follow up.

perseverō, -are, -āvī, -ātum (*v.i.*): to persist.

persolvō, -ere, -vī, -ūtum (*v.t.*): to pay.

perspiciō, -ere, -spexī, -spectum (*v.t.*): to see, see clearly, realise.

persuādeō, -ēre, -suāsī, -suāsum (*v.t.*, with *dat.*): to persuade, induce; **sibi persuaderi**: he was certain.

perterreō, -ēre, -uī, -itum (*v.t.*): to alarm, frighten thoroughly, terrify.

pertinācia, -ae (*f.*): obstinacy.

pertineō, -ēre, -uī, -tentum (*v.i.*): to stretch, reach to; to tend to, have the effect of; to have to do with, be needed for; to point to (see **eodem**).

perturbō, -āre, -āvī, -ātum (*v.t.*): to frighten, alarm, disturb.

perveniō, -īre, -vēnī, -ventum (*v.t.*): to come to, reach, arrive.

pēs, pedis (*m.*): foot; **pedem refero**: to withdraw, retreat.

petō, -ere, -īvī or -ii, -itum (*v.t.*): to seek, look for; to ask, ask for.

phalanx, -angis (*f.*): phalanx, line; close order (of fighting).

pīlum, -ī (*n.*): javelin (described in Introduction).

placeō, -ēre, -uī, -itum (*v.i.*): to please (generally in 3rd *pers.*); **placet ei**: he decides.

plānitiēs, -ēī (*f.*): level ground, plain.

plebs, plēbis (*f.*): the populace, the common people.

plērumque (*adv.*): generally, for the most part.

plūres, -a (*comp.* of **multi**): more, many, several.

plūrimum (*sup. adv.*): most, very.

plūrimus, -a, -um (*sup.* of **multus**): most.

plūs, plūris (*n.*, used as *comp.* of **multus**): more.

poena, -ae (*f.*): penalty, punishment.

polliceor, -ērī, -itus sum (*v.t.*): to promise, offer.

pōnō, -ere, posuī, positum (*v.t.*): to put, place, set; **castra pono:** to pitch camp.

pons, pontis (*m.*): bridge.

populātio, -ōnis (*f.*): ravaging, devastation.

populor, -ārī, -ātus sum (*v.t.*): to ravage, lay waste, plunder.

populus, -ī (*m.*): people.

portō, -āre, -āvī, -ātum (*v.t.*): to carry, take.

portōrium, -iī (*n.*): toll, tax on merchandise.

poscō, -ere, poposcī (*v.t.*): to demand.

possessio, -ōnis (*f.*): holding, possession, estate, lands.

possideō, -ēre, -sēdī, -sessum (*v.t.*): to occupy, hold, own.

possum, posse, potuī (*v.i.*): to be able, to be powerful.

post (*adv.*): after, afterwards; **biduo post:** two days later; (*prep.* with *acc.*): after.

posteā (*adv.*): after, afterwards.

posteāquam (*conj.*): after.

posterus, -a, -um: later, subsequent, next.

postquam (*conj.*): after.

postrīdiē (*adv.*): on the next day (often also **postridie eius diei**).

postulātum, -ī (*n.*): a demand, request.

postulō, -āre, -āvī, -ātum (*v.t.*): to ask for, demand, require.

potens, -entis (*adj.*): powerful.

potentātus, -ūs (*m.*): political supremacy, leadership.

potentia, -ae (*f.*): power.

potestās, -ātis (*f.*): power, opportunity; **potestatem facio:** offer a chance; **potestatem facere sui:** allow to approach him.

potior, -īrī, itus sum (*v.t.*, with *abl.* or *gen.*): to get possession of, to win, capture.

potius (*comp. adv.*): more, rather.

praecaveō, -ēre, -cāvī, -cautum (*v.i.*): to take precautions, guard against.

praecēdō, -ere, -cessī, -cessum (*v.t.*): to lead, excel, surpass.

praecipiō, -ere, -cēpī, -ceptum (*v.t.*): to give orders to, instruct.

praecipuē (*adv.*): especially.

praedicō, -āre, -āvī, -ātum (*v.t.*): to declare, boast.

praefectus, -ī (*m.*): officer.

praeficiō, -ere, -fēcī, -fectum (*v.t.*): to put over, put in charge of, appoint.

praemittō, -ere, -mīsī, -missum (*v.t.*): to send forward, send on.

praemium, -iī (*n.*): reward.

praeoptō, -āre, -āvī, -ātum (*v.t.*): to prefer, choose.

praepōnō, -ere, -posuī, -positum (*v.t.*): to put in charge (of).

praescrībō, -ere, -psī, -ptum (*v.t.*): to command, give orders, give instructions, dictate.

praescriptum, -i (*n.*): order, instruction.

praesens, -ntis (*adj.*): present; **in praesentia** (*acc. pl. n.*): for the present (time).

praesertim (*adv.*): especially.

praesidium, -ii (*n.*): protection, guard, bodyguard, garrison, picket; **praesidio esse**: to guard, protect.

praestō, -āre, -stitī, -stātum or **-stitum** (*v.t.* and *i.*): to excel, surpass; **praestat**: it is best.

praesum, -esse, -fuī (*v.i.*): to be at the head of, command; to hold (an office).

praeter (*prep.* with *acc.*): past beyond, besides, except, over and above.

praeterquam (*adv.*): beside; over and above, beyond.

praetereā (*adv.*): beside, further, moreover.

praeteritus, -a, -um: past.

praetor, -is (*m.*): praetor (in Rome, a judge; with the army, a senior officer); **pro praetore**: propraetor, acting praetor.

praetōrius, -a, -um: of the commander; **praetoria cohors**: bodyguard.

precēs, -um (*f. pl.*): prayer, entreaty, petition (**prex**, *nom. sing.*, not found).

premō, -ere, pressī, pressum (*v.t.*): to harass, press hard.

prendō, -ere, prendī, prensum (*v.t.*, also **prehendo**): to take, grasp, catch hold of.

pretium, -iī (*n.*): price.

prīdiē (*adv.*): the day before.

prīmō, prīmum (*adv.*): first, at first; **quam prīmum**: as soon as possible.

primus, -a, -um: first; **prima luce, nocte**: at dawn, at nightfall.

princeps, -cipis (*adj.*): first, principal; (as *n.*): chief, leader.

principātus, -ūs (*m.*): first place, leadership, chieftainship.

pristinus, -a, -um: former, ancient.

prius (*adv.*): before; **priusquam** (*conj.*) before (sometimes **prius . . . quam**).

prīvātim (*adv.*): privately, as individuals.

prīvātus, -a, -um: private, personal.

prō (*prep.* with *abl.*): for, in return for, in place of, on behalf of, in front of, in comparison with, considering; **pro praetore**: acting (as) praetor.

probō, -āre, -āvī, -ātum (*v.t.*): to prove, show clearly.

prōcēdō, -ere, -cessī, -cessum (*v.i.*): to go forward, advance.

prōcurrō, -ere, -currī, -cursum (*v.i.*): to run forward, charge.

prōdeō, -īre, -iī, -itum (*v.i.*): to go forward, come forward, advance, go.

prōdō, -ere, -didī, -ditum (*v.t.*): to hand down.

prōdūcō, -ere, -duxī, -ductum (*v.t.*): to lead forward, lead out.

proelium, -iī (*n.*): battle.

profectio, -onis (*f.*): start, departure.

prōficiō, -ere, -fēcī, -fectum (*v.t.*): to accomplish.

proficiscor, -ī, -fectus sum (*v.i.*): to start, leave, set out.

prōfugiō, -ere, -fūgī (*v.i.*): to flee, escape.

prōgredior, -ī, -gressus sum (*v.i.*): to go forward, advance.

prōhibeō, -ēre, -uī, -itum (*v.t.*): to prevent, keep out, restrain, shut off.

prōiciō, -ere, -iēcī, -iectum (*v.t.*): to cast, throw away.

prōmoveō, -ēre, -mōvī, -mōtum (*v.t.*): to move forward.

prope (*adv.*): nearly; (*prep.* with *acc.*): near.

prōpellō, -ere, -pūlī, -pulsum (*v.t.*): to drive before one, beat off.

propinquus, -a, -um: near, related; (as *noun., m.* or *f.*): a relation, kinsman, kinswoman.

propius (*comp.* of **prope,** *adv.*): nearer; (also as *prep.*, with *acc.*).

prōpōnō, -ere, -posuī, -positum (*v.t.*): to set forth, describe, explain, disclose.

propter (*prep.* with *acc.*): because of.

proptereā quod (*conj.*): for the reason that, because.

prōpulsō, -āre, -āvī, -atum (*v.t.*): to repel, drive off.

prōspiciō, -ere, -spexī, -spectum (*v.t.*): to provide for (with *dat.*).

prōvincia, -ae (*f.*): province, sphere of influence; the Province (the Roman province of South Gaul).

proximē (*sp. adv.*): most recently.

proximus, -a, -um (*sup.* of **prope**): nearest, next; (with *acc.*): nearest to; nearby, neighbouring.

publicē (*adv.*): in the name of the people, officially.

publicus, -a, -um: public; **publicae iniuriae**: wrongs done to the people.

pudor, -ōris (*m.*): shame, sense of shame; loyalty, honour; sense of honour.

puer, -erī (*m.*): boy, child.

pugna, -ae (*f.*): battle, fight, fighting.

pugnō, -āre, -āvī, -ātum (*v.i.*): to fight; **pugnatum est**: they fought, fighting went on.

purgō, -āre, -āvī, -ātum (*v.t.*): to clear (of guilt).

putō, -āre, -āvī, -ātum (*v.t.*): to think, feel, believe.

Q.: Quintus (Roman *praenomen*).

quā (*adv.*): where.

quadrāgintā (*num.*): forty.

quadringentī, -ae, -a: 400.

quaerō, -ere, quaesiī or **quaesīvī, -sītum** (*v.t.*): to ask, seek, inquire; to consider, ask oneself.

quaestor, -ōris (*m.*): quaestor (administrative officer, also employed on military duties).

quālis, -e (*rel.* or *interrog. adj.*): of what kind, (such) as; of what kind?

quam (*adv.*): how, as; with superlatives: as . . . as possible, *e.g.* **quam primum**: as soon as possible; **quam diu**: as long as; (*conj.*) than.

quamobrem (*adv.*, also as 3 words): why; for which reason, wherefore.

quantus, -a, -um: how great; as great as; **quantum**: how much.

quārē (*adv.*): why, as to why; **hortor quare**: to encourage to . . . ; (*conj.*): wherefore, for which reason, why.

quartus, -a, -um: fourth.

quattuor (*num.*): four.

-que (*enclitic conj.*): and.

quemadmodum (*adv.*): as, in whatever way; how, in what way (also as 3 words).

queror, -ī, questus sum (*v.t. and i.*): to complain, complain of, bewail.

quī ,quae, quod (*rel. pron.*): who, which, what.

quī, quae or **qua, quod** (*indef. adj.*): any.

quicumque, quaecumque, quodcumque (*rel. pron.*): whoever, whatever.

quid (*adv.*): why?

quīdam, quaedam, quoddam: a certain, certain; (*pl.*): some.

quidem (*adv.*): indeed; **ne . . . quidem**: not even.

quin (*conj.*): but that, that not; (often) that; (prevent, etc.) from . . . ing; **quin etiam**: moreover, furthermore.

quindecim (*num.*): fifteen.

quingentī, -ae, -a (*num.*): 500.

quīnī, -ae, -a (*distrib. num.*): five each, five at a time, five at any time.

quīnquāgintā (*num.*): fifty.

quīnque (*num.*): five.

quīntus, -a, -um: fifth.

quis, quid (*interrog. pron.*): who, what.

quis, quid (*indef. pron.*): anyone, anything, any.

quisquam, quidquam or **quicquam** (*indef. pron.*): anyone, anything, any (in *negs.* or *virtual negs.*).

quisque, quaeque, quodque (*indef. pron.*): each, every, all the . . .

quō (*adv.*): to any place, anywhere; whither, where; (*conj.*, with *indic.*): the more . . .; (with *subj.*): so as to . . . more . . .; **quo minus**: so as not to; **recuso quo minus** + *subj.*: refuse to.

quod (*conj.*): because, that; as for the fact that; as far as; whereas; **quod si**: but if.

quoniam (*conj.*): because, since.

quoque (*conj.* or *adv.*): also.

quotannīs (*adv.*): every year.

quotiens (*adv.*): how often; as often as, whenever.

rādix, -icis (*f.*): root, lower part, bottom (of hill).

raeda, -ae (*f.*): wagon.

rapina, -ae (*f.*): pillage, plundering.

ratio, -ōnis (*f.*): way, method; thought; reason; strategy; terms; account.

ratis, -is (*f.*): raft.

recens, -ntis: fresh, newly-won.

recipiō, -ere, -cēpī, -ceptum (*v.t.*): to take back, receive, accept; **se recipio**: to retreat, retire, withdraw, flee.

recūsō, -āre, -āvī, -ātum (*v.t.* and *i.*): to refuse, renounce; to object to, raise objections about.

reddō, -ere, -didī, -ditum
(*v.t.*): to give back.

redeō, -īre, -iī, -itum (*v.i.*):
to go back, return.

redigō, -ere, -ēgī, -actum
(*v.t.*): to reduce.

**redimō, -ere, -ēmī, -emp-
tum** (*v.t.*): to buy, buy up;
to gain, purchase.

redintegrō, -āre, -āvī, -ātum
(*v.t.*): to renew.

reditio, -ōnis (*f.*): return.

redūcō, -ere, -duxī, -ductum
(*v.t.*): to lead back, bring
back, take back.

**referō, -ferre, rettulī, relā-
tum** (*v.t.*): to bring back,
bring; to deliver; to report;
to repay; **pedem referō**:
to retreat, withdraw.

regio, -ōnis (*f.*): region, district.

regnum, -ī (*n.*): kingly power,
chieftainship.

reiciō, -ere, -iēcī, -iectum
(*v.t.*): to throw back, cast
away; to drive back.

**relinquō, -ere, -līquī, -lic-
tum** (*v.t.*): to leave, leave
behind, forsake.

reliquus, -a, -um: remaining,
left; the rest of; (in *pl.*): the
others, the rest.

**remaneō, -ēre, -mansī,
-mansum** (*v.i.*): to stay
behind.

reminiscor, -ī: to remember.

remittō, -ere, -mīsī, -missum
(*v.t.*): to send back, remit.

remōtus, -a, -um (*perf. part.
pass.* of **removeo**): far.

**removeō, -ēre, -mōvī, -mō-
tum** (*v.t.*): to remove, send
away.

remūneror, -ārī, -ātus sum
(*v.t.*): to repay, reward.

renuntiō, -āre, -āvī, -ātum
(*v.t.*): to report, tell.

**repellō, -ere, reppulī, repul-
sum** (*v.t.*): to repel, beat
back.

repentē (*adv.*): suddenly.

repentīnus, -a, -um: sudden.

**reperiō, -īre, repperī, reper-
tum** (*v.t.*): to find, get,
secure, reach.

repetō, -ere, -īvī or **-iī,
itum** (*v.t.*): to ask back;
to ask for return of; to claim.

**repraesentō, -āre, -āvī, -ā-
tum** (*v.t.*): to do immediately.

reprehendō, -ere, -dī, -sum
(*v.t.*): to blame.

repudiō, -āre, -āvī, -ātum
(*v.t.*): to reject, throw away.

repugnō, -āre, -āvī, -ātum
(*v.i.*): to oppose, be opposed
to.

res, reī (*f.*): thing, matter;
property; (in *pl.*): fortunes.
*Other meanings must come
from the context. Thus:*
rem gerere: to fight; **res
frumentaria**: supplies, provisions; **res militaris**: military matters, war; **res novae**:
a change of government;
res publica: state, government, affairs of state.

**rescindō, -ere, -scidī, -scis-
sum** (*v.t.*): to break down,
demolish.

rescīscō, -ere, -iī or **-īvī,
-ītum** (*v.t.*): to learn, find out.

rescrībō, -ere, -psī, -ptum
(*v.t.*): to transfer, remuster;
ad equum rescribo: to
transfer to the list of Knights,
to make a Knight.

reservō, -āre, -āvī, ātum
(*v.t.*): to keep, keep back.

resistō, -ere, -stitī, -stitum (*v.i.*): to resist, stand up against.

respondeō, -ēre, -dī, -sum (*v.t.*): to answer, reply.

responsum, -ī (*n.*): answer.

respuō, -ere, -uī (*v.t.*): to reject.

restituō, -ere, -uī, -ūtum (*v.t.*): to restore, rebuild.

retineō, -ēre, -uī, -tentum (*v.t.*): to keep back, restrain.

revellō, -ere, -ī, -vulsum (*v.t.*): to tear away, drag away.

revertō, -ere, -tī, -sum (*v.i.*): also *dep. vb.* **revertor, -tī, -sus sum**: to return, come back.

rex, rēgis (*m.*): king.

rīpa, -ae (*f.*): bank.

rogō, -āre, -āvī, -ātum (*v.t.*): to ask, ask for.

rota, -ae (*f.*): wheel.

rursus (*adv.*): again.

saepe (*adv.*): often; **saepe numero**: often, repeatedly.

saepius (*comp.* of **saepe**): again and again.

salūs, -ūtis (*f.*): safety.

sanciō, -īre, sanxī, sanctum (*v.t.*): to bind (by oath).

sānitās, -ātis (*f.*): good sense, reasonable frame of mind.

sarcinae, -ārum (*f.*): baggage, kit.

satis (*adv.*): enough, sufficiently, fairly; (*n.*, with *gen.*): enough of; **satis habeo**: to be satisfied.

satisfaciō, -ere, -fēcī, -factum (*v.i.*): to satisfy, apologise, give compensation.

satisfactio, -ōnis (*f.*): satisfaction, apology.

scelus, -eris (*n.*): wickedness, crime.

scientia, -ae (*f.*): knowledge.

sciō, -īre, -īvī, -ītum (*v.t.*): to know.

scūtum, -ī (*n.*): shield.

sē or **sēsē**: himself, themselves, etc.; **inter se**: each other; **se recipio**: to withdraw, retire, retreat.

sēcrētō (*adv.*): in private, secretly.

secundum (*prep.* with *acc.*): following, along, next after.

secundus, -a, -um: second, favourable; **res secundae**: prosperity.

sed (*conj.*): but.

sēdecim (*num.*): sixteen.

sēdēs, -is (*f.*): home, dwelling-place.

sēditiōsus, -a, -um: seditious, trouble-making.

semel (*adv.*): once.

sēmentis, -is (*f.*): a sowing.

semper (*adv.*): always.

senātus, -ūs (*m.*): senate.

senex, -is (*m.*): old man.

sēnī, -ae, -a (*distrib. num.*): six each.

sententia, -ae (*f.*): opinion; **in eam sententiam quare**: to show why.

sentiō, -īre, sensī, sensum (*v.t.*): to perceive, feel, realise.

separātim (*adv.*): separately.

septem (*num.*): seven.

septentrio, -ōnis (*m.*, generally in *pl.*): the North (the Great Bear, the 'seven plough-oxen').

septimus, -a, -um: seventh.

sepultūra, -ae (*f.*): burial.

sequor, -ī, secūtus sum (*v.t.*): to follow, ensue; to befall.

servīlis, -e: of a slave, of slaves.

servitūs, -ūtis (*f.*): slavery.

servus, -ī (*m.*): slave.

sescentī, -ae, -a (*num.*): 600.

sēsē = se.

sētius (*adv., comp.* of **secus**): less; **nihilo setius:** none the less.

seu = sive.

sex (*num.*): six.

sī (*conj.*): if; **si possent perrumpere:** to see if they could break through.

sīc (*adv.*): so, in this way.

sīcut (*adv.*): just as.

signum, -ī (*n.*): standard (of legion), signal, sign; **signa fero:** to march, march off, break camp; **signa infero:** to advance; **signa converto:** to face about.

silva, -ae (*f.*): wood, forest.

simul (*adv.*): at the same time, also, likewise.

simulātio, -ōnis (*f.*): pretence, pretext, excuse.

simulō, -āre, -āvī, -ātum (*v.t.*): to pretend.

sīn (*conj.*): but if.

sine (*prep.* with *abl.*): without.

singulī, -ae, -a (*distrib. num.*): one at a time, each individually; **singulis . . . singulos . . . praefecerant:** they had appointed one . . . to each . . .

sinister, -tra, -trum: left.

sinistra, -ae (*f.*): left hand, the left.

sīve (= **seu**) (*conj.*): whether, or if; **sive . . . sive:** whether . . . or . . .

socer, -ī (*m.*): father-in-law.

socius, -iī (*m.*): ally, comrade.

sōl, sōlis (*m.*): sun.

solum, -ī (*n.*): soil; **solum agri:** the ground and nothing else.

sōlum (*adv.*): only, alone.

sōlus, -a, -um: alone, only.

soror, -ōris (*f.*): sister.

sors, -rtis (*f.*): lot, casting of lots; (often in *pl.*).

spatium, -iī (*n.*): space, time, interval, distance.

speciēs, -ēī (*f.*): sight, appearance; **ad speciem:** to make his numbers seem greater.

spectō, -āre, -āvī, -ātum (*v.t.*): to look at, face, face towards; to be situated, lie; to consider, have regard for.

speculor, -ārī, -ātus sum (*v.t.*): to spy.

spērō, -āre, -āvī, -ātum (*v.t.*): to hope, hope for.

spēs, speī (*f.*): hope.

spīritus, -ūs (*m.*): pride, haughtiness, arrogance (*gen.* in *pl.*).

sponte (*fem. abl.,* with *pron. adj.:* **meā, tuā, suā**): of one's own accord, by one's own efforts, without help from others.

statim (*adv.*): at once, immediately.

statuō, -ere, -uī, -ūtum (*v.t.*): to resolve, decide; **graviter statuo in** (with *acc.*): to deal severely with.

stīpendiārius, -a, -um (can be *noun. m.*): paying tribute, tributary.

stīpendium, -iī (*n.*): tribute.

studeō, -ēre, -uī (*v.i.*): to be eager for.

studium, -iī (*n.*): keenness, enthusiasm; loyalty, devotion.

sub (*prep.* with *acc.*): under, up to; (with *abl.*): under, at the foot of; **sub septentrionibus** (under the Great Bear): towards the North.

subdūcō, -ere, -duxī, -ductum (*v.t.*): to draw off, move (troops).

subeō, -ire, -iī, -itum (*v.t.*): to go under, come under; to undergo, face.

subiciō, -ere, -iēcī, -iectum (*v.t.*): to discharge from below, throw up.

subitō (*adv.*): suddenly.

sublātus, -a, -um (see **tollo**): elated.

sublevō, -āre, -āvī, -ātum (*v.t.*): to help, relieve; **iubis equorum sublevati**: helped along by (clinging to) the horses' manes . . .

subsidium, -iī (*n.*): help, assistance.

subsistō, -ere, -stitī (*v.i.*): to halt, make a stand.

subsum, -esse, -fui (*v.i.*): to be at hand, to be near.

subtrahō, -ere, -traxī, -tractum (*v.t.*): to withdraw, take away.

subvehō, -ere, -vexī, -vectum (*v.t.*): to carry up.

succēdō, -ere, -cessī, cessum (*v.i.*): to come up, advance up to.

sum, esse, fuī (*v.i.*): to be.

summa, -ae (*f.*): the total, whole; **summa belli**: strategy, plan of campaign, conduct of the war.

sumministrō, -āre, -āvī, ātum (*v.t.*): to provide, supply.

summoveō, -ēre, -mōvī, -mōtum (*v.t.*): to drive away, drive off the field.

summus, -a, -um: highest, topmost; the top of; greatest, most important.

sūmō, -ere, sumpsī, sumptum (*v.t.*): to take, assume; **supplicium sumo de** (with *abl.*): to inflict punishment on.

sumptus, -ūs (*m.*): expense.

superbē (*adv.*): proudly.

superior, -ius (*comp.*): higher, upper.

superō, -āre, -āvī, -ātum (*v.t.*): to conquer, beat, overcome.

supersum, -esse, -fui (*v.i.*): to survive; to be left, to remain.

suppetō, -ere, -īvī (or) **ii, -ītum** (*v.i.*): to be available; to be sufficient.

suppliciter (*adv.*): humbly.

supplicium, -iī (*n.*): punishment; **supplicio adficio**: to punish (see **sumo**, above).

supportō, -āre, -āvī, -ātum (*v.t.*): to bring up.

suprā (*adv.*): above, before; (*prep.* with *acc.*): above.

suscipiō, -ere, -cēpī, -ceptum (*v.t.*): to undertake.

suspicio, -ōnis (*f.*): suspicion.

suspicor, -ārī, -ātus sum (*v.t.*): to suspect.

sustineō, -ēre, -uī, -tentum (*v.t.*): to endure, sustain; to withstand, receive (an attack).

suus, -a, -um: his own, her own, their own, etc.; **sui** (*m. pl.*): his men, their men.

T.: Titus (Roman *praenomen*).

tabernāculum, -ī (*n.*): tent.

tabula, -ae (*f.*): tablet, document, list.

taceō, -ēre, -uī, -itum (v.i.):
to be silent, say nothing;
(v.t.): to say nothing about,
conceal.

tacitus, -a, -um: silent.

tam (adv.): so.

tamen (adv.): however, yet,
nevertheless.

tametsī (conj.): although.

tandem (adv.): at last, after all.

tantopere (adv., also tantō
opere): so much, so strongly.

tantus, -a, -um: so great;
tanti (gen. of price): so
valuable, of such value.

tectum, -ī (n.): roof, house.

tēlum, -ī (n.): javelin, spear,
missile.

temerārius, -a, -um: reckless,
headstrong.

temerē (adv.): rashly; without
good reason.

temperantia, -ae (f.): moder-
ation, discretion.

temperō, -āre, -āvī, ātum
(v.i.): to refrain; temperare
sibi quin: to refrain from . . .

temptō, -āre, -āvī, -ātum
(v.t.): to try.

tempus, -oris (n.): time,
season; tam necessario
tempore: in such a crisis.

teneō, -ēre, -uī, tentum
(v.t.): to hold, restrain;
se tenere: to keep back,
stay; memoriā tenere: to
remember.

ter (adv.): thrice, three times.

tergum, -ī (n.): back; terga
vertere: to take to flight.

terra, -ae (f.): land, earth,
ground.

terrēnus, -a, -um: earthen,
of earth.

tertius, -a, -um: third.

testāmentum, -ī (n.): will.

testimōnium, -iī (n.): proof,
evidence.

testis, -is (m.): witness.

timeō, -ēre, -uī (v.t.): to fear;
(v.i.): to be afraid.

timidus, -a, -um: alarmed,
frightened.

timor, -ōris (m.): fear.

tolerō, -āre, -āvī, -ātum
(v.t.): to endure; tolero
famem: to live (on some-
thing, abl.).

tollō, -ere, sustulī, sublātum
(v.t.): to lift up, elate; to
remove, cancel.

tot (indecl. num.): so many.

totidem: as many again, as
many more.

tōtus, -a, -um: whole, entire;
the whole of.

trādō, -ere, -didī, -ditum
(v.t.): to surrender, hand over.

trāducō, -ere, -duxī, -duc-
tum (v.t.): to lead across,
bring over, to lead through,
to lead past.

trāgula, -ae (f.): javelin, dart
(used by Gauls and Span-
iards).

trahō, -ere, -xī, -ctum (v.t.):
to drag.

trānō, -āre, -āvī, -ātum (v.t.
or i.): to swim across.

trans (prep. with acc.): across,
over.

transeō, -ire, -iī, -itum (v.t.):
to go over, cross.

transfīgō, -ere, -fixī, -fixum
(v.t.): to pierce.

transportō, -āre, -āvī, -ātum
(v.t.): to bring over, trans-
port.

trēs, tria (num.): three.

tribūnus, -i (m.): tribune;
tribunus militum: military
tribune.

tribuō, -ere, -uī, -ūtum (*v.t.*): to ascribe, grant; to give credit (see **magnopere**).

triduum, -ī (*n.*): (period of) three days.

trīnī, -ae, -a (*distrib. num.*): three each; triple, threefold.

triplex, -plicis: triple, three-fold.

tristis, -e: gloomy, sorrowful.

tristitia, -ae (*f.*): sorrow, gloom.

tum (*adv.*): then.

tumultus, -ūs (*m.*): rising, revolt.

tumulus, -ī (*m.*): mound, hillock.

turpis, -e: disgraceful, shameful.

ubi (*adv., conj.*): where, when, as soon as.

ulciscor, -ī, ultus sum (*v.t.*): to punish, avenge.

ullus, -a, -um: any.

ulterior, -us: further, outer.

ultrā (*prep.* with *acc.*): beyond.

ultrō (*adv.*): beyond (expectations, etc.); of his own accord; **ultro citroque**: backwards and forwards, hither and thither.

umquam (*adv.*): ever.

unā (*adv.*): at the same time, together (often with **cum**).

unde (*adv.*): whence, from where.

undique (*adv.*): from all sides.

ūnus, -a, -um (*num.*): one, only, alone.

urbs, -is (*f.*): city; the capital, Rome.

usque (*adv.*): all the way; **usque ad**: right up to.

ūsus, -ūs (*m.*): use, experience, advantage; **usui esse**: to be useful; **ex usu esse**: to be advantageous.

ūsus, -a, -um: see **ūtor**.

ut (*adv.* or *conj.*): how, as, when; as though; so that, so as to, (so . . .) that, to . . .; **timeo ut**: to fear that . . . not (= **ne non**).

uter, utra, utrum: which (of two).

uterque, utraque, utrumque: both, each.

utī = ut.

ūtor, -ī, ūsus sum (*v.i.* with *abl.*): to use, follow, employ, apply, enjoy, show; **qua multa utebatur** (*i.e.* lingua): which he spoke well.

utrimque (*adv.*): on each side, on both sides.

utrum (*adv.*): whether.

uxor, -ōris (*f.*): wife.

V.: five, fifth.

vacō, -āre, -āvī, -ātum (*v.i.*): to be empty; to be uninhabited.

vadum, -ī (*n.*): ford.

vagor, -ārī, -ātus sum (*v.i.*): to wander, rove.

valeō, -ēre, -uī (*v.i.*): to be strong, to be important; to prevail, be stronger.

vallum, -ī (*n.*): palisade, rampart, defence-work.

vastō, -āre, āvī, -ātum (*v.t.*): to lay waste, devastate.

vāticinātio, -ōnis (*f.*): soothsaying.

-ve (*enclitic particle*): or.

vectigal, -ālis (*n.*): tax, tribute.

vectus, -a, -um: see **veho**.

vehementer (*adv.*): strongly, seriously, violently.

vehō, -ere, vexī, -vectum
(*v.t.*): to convey, carry;
equo vehor: to ride.
vel (*conj.*): or; **vel . . . vel:**
either . . . or . . .
vēlox, -ōcis: swift, quick.
velut (*adv.*): just as . . .
veniō, īre, vēnī, ventum
(*v.i.*): to come; **venio in
spem:** to have hopes, to
hope.
verbum, -ī (*n.*): word.
vereor, -ērī, -itus sum (*v.t.*):
to fear, to be afraid.
vergō, -ere (*v.i.*): to stretch
towards, be situated; to
face.
vērō (*adv.*): in truth, however,
but.
versō, -āre, -āvī, -ātum (*v.t.*):
to keep turning, turn about;
(often in *pass.*): to take part
in, be engaged in.
vertō, -ere, -tī, -sum (*v.t.*):
to turn.
vērus, -a, -um: true.
vesper, -eris and **-erī** (*m.*):
evening.
veterānus, -a, -um (often as
noun. m.): veteran.
vetus, -eris (*adj.*): ancient,
old.
vexō, -āre, -āvī, -ātum (*v.t.*):
to injure, molest, annoy,
harass, ravage.
via, -ae (*f.*): route, way,
journey.
victor, -ōris (*m.*, or *adj.*):
victor, conqueror; victorious.
victōria, -ae (*f.*): victory.
victus, -ūs (*m.*): living, way of
life.
victus, -a, -um (*perf. pass.
part.* of **vinco**): beaten,
conquered.
vīcus, -ī (*m.*): village.

videō, -ēre, vīdī, vīsum
(*v.t.*): to see; (in *pass.*,
generally but not always):
to seem, appear.
vigilia, -ae (*f.*): watch; watch
(as one-quarter of the night-
time).
vīgintī (*num.*): twenty.
vinciō, -ire, -nxī, -nctum
(*v.t.*): to bind, put in chains.
vinclum, -ī (*n.*, also **vincu-
lum**): chain, fetter.
vincō, -ere, vīcī, victum
(*v.t.*): to defeat, beat, conquer.
virtūs, -ūtis (*f.*): virtue,
bravery.
vīs, vim, vī (*pl.* **vīres**) (*f.*):
violence, force; attack; (*pl.*):
strength.
vīta, -ae (*f.*): life.
vīto, -āre, -āvī, -ātum (*v.t.*):
to avoid.
vix (*adv.*): scarcely, hardly;
with difficulty.
vocō, āre, -āvī, -ātum (*v.t.*):
to call, summon, send for.
volō, velle, voluī (*v.t.* and
i.): to wish, to be willing; to
mean, intend (often with **sibi**).
voluntās, -ātis (*f.*): will, wish;
goodwill, freewill, permission.
voluptās, -ātis (*f.*): pleasure.
vox, vōcis (*f.*): voice, sound,
speech; (in *pl.*): talk.
vulgus, -ī (*n.*, rarely *m.*):
the common people, popu-
lace; the general mass; **vulgō:**
generally, all over (the camp).
vulnerō, -āre, -āvī, -ātum
(*v.t.*): to wound, strike.
vulnus, -eris (*n.*): wound.
vultus, -ūs (*m.*): face, expression; **vultum fingo:** to
feign one's expression, pretend to be cheerful.